MW00718424

ENTREPRENEUR:
A SIMULATION

ENTREPRENEUR: A SIMULATION

Jerald R. Smith
University of Louisville

Peggy A. Golden
University of Louisville

Houghton Mifflin Company   Boston

Dallas   Geneva, Illinois   Palo Alto   Princeton, New Jersey

Cover Photo by Michel Tcherevkoff.

Copyright © 1987 by Houghton Mifflin Company. All Rights
Reserved.

No part of this work may be reproduced or transmitted in any
form or by any means, electronic or mechanical, including
photocopying and recording, or by any information storage
or retrieval system, except as may be expressly permitted by
the 1976 Copyright Act or in writing by the Publisher.
Requests for permission should be addressed to Permissions,
Houghton Mifflin Company, One Beacon Street, Boston,
Massachusetts 02108.

Printed in the U.S.A.

ISBN: 0-395-45302 X

K-QF-0987654321

CONTENTS

PREFACE

Entrepreneur: A Simulation is a dynamic business exercise designed for students enrolled in any type of course that features the concepts of business and management. It provides student players with simulated real-world experience in managing the variables that are encountered in business decision making. It enables the student to practice various principles in addition to learning them — a learning-by-doing approach to education.

The scenario and the rules of the simulation can be learned in less than an hour. Two important benefits for players of the simulation are the experience early in their educational process of just how many areas of business are interrelated and the demonstration that the decision maker must consider how each area affects the others. Although the scenario described pertains to the retail clothing industry, the instructor can substitute another scenario.

Briefly, the simulation involves the takeover and continuing operation of a retail clothing store. In playing the simulation, students acting as management teams make a variety of decisions that will have an impact on their store's operations. These decisions include selection of the type of merchandise that will be carried — students may choose among five different clothing product lines: modern, designer, regional/ethnic, very contemporary, and professional uniforms. Players must establish prices for pants/jeans as well as tops/blouses. The amount of the advertising and sales promotion expenditure must be determined and the size of the sales force established. Inventory management is an important element of the simulation, and teams must determine how much clothing to purchase each decision period. Selecting the appropriate market research study can aid in compiling decision data. A unique feature of the simulation is the inclusion of environmental and social responsibility incidents that the business faces in each decision period.

Student decisions are inputted on a microcomputer and results are available within minutes. Students analyze the printout that is produced each decision period, agree on a new set of decisions, and input these. Each decision period is assumed to be one quarter (3 months).

The objectives of *Entrepreneur: A Simulation* are:

1. To allow students with different academic interests to make business decisions after considering the multidimensional aspects of the decisions.
2. To provide the opportunity for student interaction in organizational teamwork.
3. To allow students to practice their communication, leadership, and interpersonal relations skills.
4. To aid in developing logical and rational decision-making skills.
5. To demonstrate the importance of management information tools.
6. To introduce the student to the various environmental, ethical, and social responsibility problems that may occur in a firm and to show the consequences of the decisions that are made.

Unfortunately, no simulation can duplicate real life — the latter is much too complicated for that! However, this simulation will allow the student to plan, organize, direct, and control a business enterprise using a model that is as close as possible to actual conditions.

The instructor is provided with an Instructor's Manual that explains how to administer the simulation and offers suggestions for grading the performance of student teams. The program disk is provided to bona fide adopters of the student manual. The instructor needs no computer knowledge to administer the simulation.

ACKNOWLEDGMENTS

We are grateful to all those who have supported the simulation development process. A special thanks goes to all the users of earlier simulation games who have provided feedback and guidance in the development of this new experience. The Houghton Mifflin staff deserve praise for their continuous encouragement and support of our efforts. We appreciate the Dean of the University of Louisville School of Business, Bob Taylor, and the Management faculty for their insights and help in conceptualizing, writing, and program development. Special thanks go to the Word Processing Center and Denice Nance for her tireless patience with changes in the text.

Finally, our thanks go to our families for their patience with the long working days and nights that go into simulation development.

Jerald R. Smith
Peggy A. Golden

1
THE SIMULATION SCENARIO

INTRODUCTION TO SIMULATION

Welcome to the exciting world of simulation! Unlike most classroom exercises, a simulation provides an opportunity for continuous practice in managing an organization. The student has the unique opportunity to make decisions, see how the decisions work out, and then try again! Thus, students get hands-on experience manipulating key business variables in a dynamic setting.

Simulation techniques have been used for some time in the attempt to create business models that can aid in explaining the real world. In this simulation we have attempted to combine the marketing reactions found in the real world with the business environment found in this type of competitive situation. This model will take the decisions each team makes and simulate consumers' reaction. The relative "appropriateness" of each team's decisions will be reported on the team's financial report.

In the real world, managers must make decisions without perfect information, under conditions of uncertainty, and under time constraints. This simulation is no different! You will need to get as much information as possible through the market research reports provided, keep good records in order to study the interactions among the marketing variables, and then make your decisions for the next round. It is recommended that you do not use the "stab in the dark" method of making decisions. Plan instead to hold certain variables constant while manipulating others. This procedure will allow you to begin to determine which marketing elements are more effective in generating sales. Do NOT rely on information gathered from others who have competed in the simulation in the past as instructors can change the competitive environment of the simulation for each class!

Each company in this simulation is composed of one to four class members who assume responsibility for the operation of their assigned firm. The organizing of individual teams is normally left up to each team by the instructor. Your company will be competing with other teams (up to 20 total) in the dynamic retail clothing business. Teams are expected to establish objectives, plan their strategy, and then make the required business decisions dictated by these plans. Decisions are submitted to the instructor periodically. These decisions are entered into the computer, which produces a report for each team concerning the firm's sales and profits. This is done for several iterations. It is strongly recommended that student teams approach the simulation as a real-world

© 1987 Houghton Mifflin Company

competition against other firms and not attempt to play "against" the computer. All teams will make a few mistakes during the simulation, so don't allow a few setbacks to affect your play—mistakes happen in the real world too! Keep your spirits up and good luck!

THE RETAIL CLOTHING INDUSTRY AND YOUR SIMULATION ENVIRONMENT

The tops and slacks store that you will be establishing and operating is a specialty business in the retail apparel industry. This specialty grew quickly in the late 1960s when casual clothing became universally adopted as acceptable attire. Merchants recognized that purchasers of slacks and tops crossed age, sex, socioeconomic, and international boundaries. Although the early entrants in this market limited their inventory to jeans, most successful operations have broadened their inventory to include a variety of styles of pants and tops (slacks, fatigues, T-shirts, blouses, casual shirts, etc.). This selection provides a more complete product mix to customers.

Stores that sell slacks and tops can be found in a variety of locations. Although they are most evident in retail malls, successful operations can be found in shopping plazas, downtown stores, and other types of retail space (e.g., adjacent to convenience grocery stores, abandoned gas stations, and hotel arcades). Each type of location attracts a unique clientele, and it is important to be able to identify the population your store is serving and to determine whether there is a large enough segment available to generate profits.

The type of population, or market segment, affects the type of inventory carried in an individual store. Retailers report that they carry anywhere from two to six types of slacks and an equivalent array of tops, depending on the clientele they wish to attract.

The average floor space required for this type of retail outlet is 3,000 square feet with additional stockroom space of 2,000 to 2,500 square feet. Retail slacks and tops outlets of this size usually have a sales force of two persons at all times except for weekend afternoons and peak seasons, such as "back-to-school" and Christmas rush, when three salespersons are necessary. Staffing also includes a manager or assistant manager at all times. Productivity of retail outlets can be measured either by sales per square foot or sales per payroll dollar.

© 1987 Houghton Mifflin Company

Markup on inventory usually averages 100%; this means if the wholesale cost of the item is $10, the retail price will be $20. End-of-season reductions run approximately 25–35%, causing narrow profit margins on sale merchandise. Outlets of this type occasionally take advantage of buyouts of job lots and pass the savings on to the customers at the same profit margins as the regular stock. These are commonly advertised as "special buys." Jeans and slacks are the more popular product, with approximately three units sold for each top sold. This is due to the fact that jeans/slacks are a universal item, while tops have specific market segment appeal.

Retail apparel outlets advertise their merchandise in a number of ways. The most common is newspaper advertising that is prepared by an agency and paid for as an expense of the business. In addition, the manufacturer may provide co-op advertising if the retail outlet is carrying an item that the manufacturer selects for promotion.

Advertising of this type, which promotes the item rather than the store, can save the retailer about 50% in advertising costs and provides a residual image to consumers. When Levi Strauss promotes a new line of jeans and announces that they can be purchased at a specified outlet, this is an example of co-op advertising. Some shopping centers include "flyer" advertising as a benefit of tenancy; other shopping centers require that tenants participate in mall promotions and charge tenants for the advertising. Clothing retailers are able to reach their target segments effectively through this kind of flyer if they have chosen their location wisely.

Other forms of advertising are effective only if the medium is chosen carefully for its *reach/cost* relationship. All media are able to provide information on their audience and a price list that is differentiated by time of day and audience.

The small retail clothing store is a stable segment of the retail clothing business that can be organized and operated profitably if managed efficiently and effectively. It tends to be adaptable to many types of locations and can be stocked with a variety of types of clothing. These decisions and many others challenge the entrepreneur who wishes to operate this type of business for a profit! This simulation will allow you to try your hand at managing a retail specialty clothing store without having to invest the actual money and to make mistakes without costing any money!

© 1987 Houghton Mifflin Company

YOUR STORE

The store you are buying out has a long history in your local community. It has been a family-owned business for many years, selling casual tops and pants for work and recreation. The youngest members of the family have pursued careers in high-tech fields, and the retiring owners are interested in selling the business to ambitious entrepreneurs who can update the image and carry the business forward.

Although the line of clothing carried by the store at this time may not be your preference, the specific line can be changed during the first decision period. The store's relationship with suppliers is excellent, and a primary vendor has offered to buy back the existing stock if you purchase a different line through them. Since the store has always closed for a one-week vacation, you can spruce up and restock with merchandise of your own choice without disrupting service to existing customers.

Your accountant has audited the books and believes that the business is a healthy going concern, although it could be operated more efficiently than the previous owners have been doing. In her opinion, the purchase price of $55,000 is fair since it includes goodwill, some residual advertising, and a small start-up inventory. Your team has formed a corporation and has "pooled resources" of $40,000 that will become the equity in the business. (Common stock will be issued for $40,000.)

The remaining cost will be financed with a note from a local bank that has a reputation for supporting new business ventures such as yours. A consultant from the local office of the Small Business Administration has indicated that a $25,000 loan will cover the remaining start-up expenses and provide some initial working capital.

The business has three months left on its lease. You can either continue in the present location next to a convenience grocery store near a university campus or move to a nearby small shopping center that is surrounded by newly developed houses and apartment complexes. The rent in the university location is $14,800 annually ($3,700 quarterly); the rent in the shopping center is $24,000 annually ($6,000 quarterly). The rent at both locations includes exterior maintenance. The shopping center location includes some free flyer advertising and has a bit more walk-by traffic than does the current location. Owners of both locations require a $10,000 damage and rent prepayment deposit.

© 1987 Houghton Mifflin Company

Your store has the option of carrying five (5) different lines of moderately priced slacks and tops. The product line should be carefully selected to appeal to the customers in the location you have selected. Your product line may be changed during the simulation with the permission of your instructor.

The industry average selling price for this type of line of slacks is $19.95; the tops sell for an average of $11.95. For the purposes of the simulation, you must specify one price for slacks and one price for tops in any given quarter. These are average prices for the quarter; this average includes some lower-priced goods and some higher-priced goods. It also reflects any special sales, promotional activities, and discount policies.

Some stores such as yours conduct their business on a cash basis only, while others accept bank credit cards as well. All sales transactions will produce cash to meet expenses in the quarter in which they are sold. If you choose to accept credit cards, the bank will charge a fee of 4% on all credit card purchases and the simulation will assume that 50% of your sales are credit card sales. Therefore, you will be charged a 4% service fee on 50% of your sales each quarter. (For example, if you have sales of $60,000, the bank will charge 4% of $30,000, or $1,200.) There is some evidence that credit card customers make somewhat larger purchases; however, this may or may not offset the fee.

You must pay for your purchases when they are ordered, which may cause your checking account balance to get very low. The local bank has indicated that it will grant you loans for working capital at its usual lending rate of 12%. Loans will be granted automatically if you overdraw your checking account. In order to provide this service, the bank requires a $2,000 balance, so an overdraft loan will be made in an amount to bring your account to $2,000. Any cash in excess of $2,000 will be automatically invested in investments. Interest will be paid at 2/3 of the current loan interest rate. At the beginning of the simulation, investments pay 8% per year, or 2% quarterly (2/3 x 12%).

You will make decisions on a quarterly basis and receive a printed report that indicates your performance for the quarter just ended. The first set of decisions will include your selection of an appropriate site. You may make this decision only once.

© 1987 Houghton Mifflin Company

2

DECISION MAKING AND REPORTING

This chapter contains the information needed to complete your first decision form and to interpret the results shown on the quarterly report. Decision forms are found at the back of the book. Quarterly reports are generated each time a team's decisions are inputted into the computer. Figure 2.1, which follows the explanation of all decisions, shows a completed decision form.

THE DECISION-MAKING PROCESS

Purchasing Inventory

Your team must decide what quantity of slacks and tops to purchase each quarter. While you want to carry enough merchandise to display your goods in an attractive manner at all times, too much inventory will not only stretch your finances but can also result in goods that look shopworn. Overstocking would require you to hold clearance sales, which greatly dilute your profit margins. In addition, excess merchandise has a greater chance of being damaged or going out of style. It is suggested that you have about 1,200–1,500 pair of slacks and 750–1,000 tops at all times. Your first order should include approximately 3,000 pair of slacks. This amount is enough to build up your stock to an optimal level and ensure that you will have enough merchandise to meet the coming quarter's sales. You should purchase approximately 1,000 tops.

These levels of inventory will be sufficient for a normal operating quarter. Of course, sales will vary in response to the level of advertising and promotion, the relative price of your goods as compared to your competitors', and the business environment as indicated by the Business Index (shown on the quarterly report). You will need to adjust your order each quarter after considering these factors. Place the number of slacks and tops ordered on lines 1 and 2 of the decision form. Your suppliers require that you order in lots of 100. You currently have 1,250 pants and 580 tops in inventory.

Type of Goods Carried

Your team has a choice of several types of clothing, ranging from uniforms for health-care and food-service professionals to ultratrendy pants and tops. There is no intention for any of the product lines to be a poor choice. Many of the product lines appear to compete for the same

© 1987 Houghton Mifflin Company

customers. For example, a customer may buy khaki slacks from you and go to another similar store for designer jeans.

Your product choice establishes a motif for your store. A trendy store might choose to play rock music and have special lighting, while a uniform store might have displays showing professionals in their work environment. You may change your product line at the beginning of each quarter. However, if you abandon a line of clothing, you will be charged $5,000 to cover the cost of converting your merchandise to new lines.

Table 2.1 shows the available clothing lines and their descriptions:

TABLE 2.1 PRODUCT TYPE

Product Line No.	Description
1	Specialty clothing of regional or ethnic interest—for example, Western, Oriental, European, "soul," etc.
2	Modern line generally found in sportswear section of department stores; includes jeans, sweaters, etc.
3	Designer line with labels and logos displayed on outside of garment
4	Ultratrendy line including fad clothing, high fashion
5	Uniforms for health-care and food-service professionals; includes a casual line of surgical scrubs

You must specify your product line type on line 3 of the decision form.

Price

All product lines cost the same unit price at the beginning of the simulation: $10 for slacks and $6 for tops. They sell for an industry average price of $19.95 for the slacks and $11.95 for the tops. These selling prices are examples and may vary from one locale to another. One general statement about pricing should be made. If a company lowers its price below that of the competition, its sales volume will increase somewhat. However, there is a point at which the revenues at the reduced price will not make up for the volume created by heavily discounted

© 1987 Houghton Mifflin Company

prices. At the other extreme, higher than usual prices may reduce sales somewhat but yield a better profit on each unit sold. The optimal price depends on the clientele, the behavior of competitors, and some factors of consumer behavior that are difficult to predict.

Companies are encouraged to experiment with selling prices to find the best pricing policy for them. The price for the quarter should reflect any sales or promotions. It is common practice to use cents in the pricing structure, since some customers believe that $xx.95 represents a better value than the next whole dollar. Enter your average selling price for slacks and tops on lines 4 and 5 of the decision form. You must enter a product type and a price for slacks and tops even if you do not purchase inventory.

Advertising and Sales Promotion

Advertising is one part of marketing that lures customers into a specific store. The subtle influences that affect consumer behavior are called "pull" marketing strategies. Stores such as yours advertise in a variety of media, such as local radio and television, newspapers (campus and daily), and home-delivered flyers. Each medium reaches different customers, but all are intended to establish your store's presence in the community and give you a better image. The cost of various types of media vary based on how many people they reach effectively.

Table 2.2 shows examples of quarterly costs and frequency of your message for various types of media.

TABLE 2.2 MEDIA COSTS

Media	Frequency	Reach	Cost/Quarter
Radio	60 seconds 3 times per week	Broad cross-section	$3,120
Television	30 seconds 2 times per week	Afternoon view/ nat'l network	$3,120
Newspaper— community	1/8 page each Sunday	Entire community	$6,000
Newspaper— campus	1/4 page 2 times per week	Students/ faculty	$2,600
Flyers	Weekly	Shopping area	$4,550

© 1987 Houghton Mifflin Company

You may choose to advertise in a specific medium for only a portion of a quarter. For example, you may choose to advertise every other week in the Sunday paper. This would cost half the amount specified in the table. You may select any combination of media for your store. There is a fine line betwen not enough advertising and too much. Your customers will be unaware of your store if you do not broadcast your presence sufficiently; on the other hand, too much advertising will erode your profits without generating the marginal dollar of new business. Advertising budgets in this industry range from 5% to 10% of gross sales.

Sales promotion is known as a "push" marketing strategy. Typical promotional activities include coupons and attractive point-of-sale displays that push merchandise into a customer's hands. The costs vary from an in-store window display designed by one of the owners and costing approximately $300 for supplies to coupon programs costing $2,000–$6,000 (depending on the value of the coupon and the response). Most retailers use a combination of advertising and sales promotions. Your advertising and promotion budget should be entered on line 6 of the decision form.

Part-time Labor Costs

Your store normally has two people on the premises at all times. This number includes someone from the management team and one additional employee. The store is open 70 hours per week and your normal labor costs are $8,000 per quarter for a manager's (or manager/owner's) salary plus $7,000 per quarter for one salesperson on the floor at all times. Thus, you will automatically be charged $15,000 per quarter for salaries and wages. In addition, you may hire part-time help for peak hours (evenings and weekends) and seasonal business such as the December holiday season and the preschool summer quarter. Part-time employees receive $450 per hour and typically work 15 hours per week. For simplicity, you only need to schedule the *number* of part-time employees desired. It is assumed that each will work 15 hours. Therefore, each added part-time employee will cost $900 per quarter. Enter the number of *additional* 15-hour-per-week part-time employees on line 7 of the decison form.

Payment for Goods Sold

The previous owners conducted all of their business on a cash basis. There is some evidence that sales may increase somewhat if bank credit

© 1987 Houghton Mifflin Company

cards (e.g., VISA, MasterCard) are used. However, banks charge stores for processing these transactions and providing prompt payment. An industry study reports that stores accepting this type of credit card have about 50% charge sales. Your bank charges you a 4% fee based on 50% of gross sales for the quarter for bank charge cards. Enter a 0 (zero) for cash only or a 1 (one) for combination cash and bank cards on line 8 of the decision form.

Market Research

Demand for products is generated by a precise mix of the correct product, attractive price, ample advertising and promotion, and a favorable economic environment. The simulation will provide information about the economic environment in the form of a Business Index at no cost to you. A market research firm has conducted studies of the local casual clothing stores and will sell current information to you as needed. The following studies are available:

1. An estimate of the average sales for the current quarter, listed in units of slacks and tops—cost $100
2. An estimate of the average advertising levels for the current quarter—cost $200
3. Average price for slacks and tops listed by product type carried—cost $400

Add the total dollars spent on market research and place that total on line 9 of the decision form. For example, if you want studies 1 and 3, place $500 on line 9 of the decision form.

DIVIDENDS

Dividends are a payment to stockholders for the investment they have made in the firm. Since the stockholders are the *owners* of a company, they have every right to be rewarded for the risk they have taken by investing capital funds in a firm. On the other hand, the firm may be in a high-growth period and need all available profits for growth purposes. It is difficult to know if the firm needs the dividends more than the stockholders do. If the firm does not have a ready use for profits, then it should pay the profits to the rightful owners—the stockholders. Many firms use the rule of thumb that says that the company should retain 50% of net profits and pay 50% of net profits to the stockholders.

© 1987 Houghton Mifflin Company

However, in a closely held company, the dividend rate might be much higher. Whatever you decide to do, always pay a dividend *quarterly* rather than once or twice a year—this is the standard practice for most firms and it makes the cash flow easier to predict.

Table 2.3 will give you some idea of the *return on investment* generated by a certain amount of dividends. Note that the annualized return assumes the given dividend payment for four consecutive quarters.

TABLE 2.3 DIVIDENDS

Amount of Stock Outstanding	Quarterly Dividend Paid	Return on Stockholder's Investment (annualized)
$40,000	$1,000	10%
40,000	2,000	20%
40,000	4,000	40%
40,000	8,000	80%

To declare a dividend, place the amount of dollars you wish to pay on line 10 of the decision form. If the dividend you want to pay is greater than the profits in a quarter, the computer will automatically adjust the dividend payment to an amount equal to that quarter's profits.

Incident Response

You should respond to the incidents in Chapter 3 by placing the number of the response your team selects on the decision form for the corresponding quarter. You may receive some type of feedback on your printout indicating how your response affected your firm. The effect on your firm has been programmed into the model from experience and probabilities found in the real world. Incident 1 is required for the simulation; your instructor will advise you concerning the use of subsequent incidents. Place your response for Incident 1 on line 11 of the decision form.

Verification Total

After you have completed the decision form, add up all of the numbers and place the total in the Verification Total box. This number may look

© 1987 Houghton Mifflin Company

strange in terms of its value, but it provides an error check for the person who enters your decisions into the computer. If you add the numbers incorrectly, it slows the process down greatly; in this case, you may expect a fine.

© 1987 Houghton Mifflin Company

FIGURE 2.1 A SAMPLE DECISION FORM FOR QUARTER 0

The decision form below has been filled out for Quarter 0.

DECISION FORM

INDUSTRY ___*A*___   QUARTER NO. ___*0*___   COMPANY NO. ___*X*___

1. Purchase # slacks (no commas)	*3000*
2. Purchase # tops (no commas)	*1000*
3. Line of clothing (1–5)	*2*
4. Price: slacks	*19.95*
5. Price: tops	*11.95*
6. Advertising & promotion (no commas)	*5000*
7. Part-time sales staff (0–10)	*0*
8. Cash only (0); Cash & credit cards (1)	*0*
9. Market research (0–$700)	*700*
10. Dividends	*500*
11. Incident	*0*
VERIFICATION TOTAL	*10,233.90*

****

Note. Add all the numbers you have inserted on lines 1 to 11. Place the total (including cents) in the verification box. This is used to verify correctness of the numbers as they are typed into the computer. The total MUST be correct or your instructor may fine you.

Members of the team present:

_____   _____

_____   _____

© 1987 Houghton Mifflin Company

Naming Your Business

One of the most important decisions an entrepreneur makes is the naming of the business. This is also a legal issue since names are ordinarily registered in the state in which the business operates (usually with the office of the secretary of state).

Once your store has a new name, the image and reputation of the store begin to take form immediately. Although you could rename a business if the first name you selected was unsatisfactory, it is important to select a name that will stand the test of time and that can perhaps even be adapted to a new product line if you desire to change the product line sometime during the simulation play.

Some factors you may want to take into consideration in naming your business and some right/wrong examples are:

1. Is the name descriptive of what you sell?
    Better: Campus Clothing Corner
    Poorer: The Corner Store
2. Is the name descriptive of your product?
    Better: Designer Jeans Depot
    Poorer: Art's Apparel
3. Is the name an ego trip? Does it contain meaningless names/words representing the owners?
    Better: The Jeans Shop
    Poorer: Peggy A. Golden's Rainbow,
    The JGD Shop (first initials of the owners), or We Three
4. Is the name distinctive, perhaps catchy, and easy to remember? Will it be conducive to future advertising jingles and logos?
    Better: Jerry's Jazzy Jeans
    Poorer: Larry Lanahan's Clothing and Department Store
5. Does the name lend itself to future changes in products or expansion of the product line (for example, accessories and shoes)?
    Better: Casual Clothes Etc.
    Poorer: Peggy's Pants

Of course, some choices are not so clear cut. Is Jerry's Jazzy Jeans primarily an ego trip, or is it easy to remember? You will need to determine which factors are most important for your team's success. Form 2.1 on page 17 may aid in selecting a name.

© 1987 Houghton Mifflin Company

FORM 2.1 NAMING YOUR BUSINESS

INDUSTRY _____   COMPANY NO. _____

This form should be completed and turned in to your instructor with the decision for the first quarter.

1. List your store's product line: _____
    _____

2. List other products you think you might want to add in the future, if any:
    _____

3. Describe your "target market" (the demographics of the segment of the population you want to serve): _____
    _____
    _____

4. List some advertising mottoes, jingles, or lines to which your target market might relate: _____
    _____
    _____
    _____

5. Describe the motif (internal decoration) you are going to use in your store: ____
    _____
    _____
    _____

6. Describe any other factors that you want to consider in naming your store: ____
    _____
    _____
    _____

7. From the data assembled above, write at least four possible names:
    a. _____
    b. _____
    c. _____
    d. _____

8. Select the best name and describe the overriding reason for its selection: _____
    _____
    _____
    _____
    _____
    _____

© 1987 Houghton Mifflin Company

ANALYZING THE QUARTERLY REPORT

Your team will receive a report at the end of each quarter similar to the one in Figure 2.2. It is important to note that Figure 2.2, Printout of the Quarterly Report, shows the quarterly results of the firm you are buying out. Since you are not purchasing their corporation but are buying only the merchandise inventory and goodwill of the store, the assets Cash and Investments shown on the balance sheet portion of the quarterly report DO NOT go with the sale.

The printout you receive when you input your team's decisions (recorded on that quarter's decision form) is divided into five sections: Income & Expense Statement, Balance Sheet, Inventory Analysis, Market Research, and News & Messages. The information in each of these sections is analyzed below.

Income & Expense Statement

The top left portion of the quarterly report is an income and expense statement for the quarter calculated on the basis of your decisions. Your quarterly profits reflect only the revenue generated by the items you actually sold during the quarter. However, since your suppliers do not sell on credit and you must pay for all goods ordered each quarter, your cash balance (accounts at the bank) will be charged with all of the goods ordered during the quarter.

Taxes and Insurance. Payroll taxes are calculated at 10% of total salaries and wages. This amount includes the employer's portion of social security and unemployment insurance. Insurance costs of $900 per quarter include fire protection, personal liability, and workers' compensation (injury), plus group life and disability insurance (for full-time employees only). In addition, $200 per month or $600 per quarter will be charged for telephone services and Yellow Pages advertising. These two expenses will be totaled on the report ($1,500 per quarter).

Your income and other taxes are calculated at 30% of any quarterly profits. This includes all federal, state, and local taxes other than payroll taxes. Sales taxes are not considered in this simulation because different states have different sales tax laws.

Interest Payments. The interest on your loan is calculated by multiplying your total outstanding loan balance by 3% (this is the quarterly

© 1987 Houghton Mifflin Company

FIGURE 2.2 PRINTOUT OF THE QUARTERLY REPORT

PERIOD 0: QUARTERLY REPORT

INDUSTRY A   CAMPUS CLOTHES CORNER   COMPANY NO. 1

INCOME & EXPENSE STATEMENT			BALANCE SHEET	
SALES – PANTS: 2700 PAIR @ 19.95	53,865			
COST OF GOODS SOLD @ 10.00	27,000			
GROSS MARGIN ON PANTS		26,865	CASH	2,000
SALES – TOPS: 900 UNITS @ 11.95	10,755		INVESTMENTS	29,000
COST OF GOODS SOLD @ 6.00	5,400		RENT DEPOSIT	10,000
GROSS MARGIN OF TOPS		5,355	INVENTORY	15,980
INTEREST INCOME		0		
NET REVENUE		32,220	TOTAL ASSETS	56,980
EXPENSES:				
ADVERTISING & PROMOTION	5,000		LOANS PAYABLE	0
MANAGER'S SALARY	8,000			
WAGES OF HOURLY WORKERS	7,000		COMMON STOCK	10,000
PAYROLL TAXES	1,500		RETAINED EARNINGS	46,980
RENT AND UTILITIES	3,700			
INSURANCE & TELEPHONE	1,500		TOT OWNER'S EQUITY	56,980
INTEREST EXPENSE	0			
BANK CHARGES	0		TOT LIAB & EQUITY	56,980
OTHER EXPENSES	0			
MKT RESEARCH	700			
SHRINKAGE COST	720			
INCOME & OTHER TAXES	1,230			
TOTAL EXPENSES	29,350			
QUARTERLY PROFITS		2,870		
LOAN REPAYMENT	0			
LOAN ADDITION	0			
DIVIDENDS PAID	500			
NET RECEIPTS THIS QTR		2,370		

*** INVENTORY ANALYSIS ***

	BEGINNING INVENTORY	PRODUCTS ORDERED	AVAILABLE FOR SALE	LESS SHRINKAGE	LESS SALES	ENDING INVENTORY
PANTS:	1000	3000	4000	50	2700	1250
TOPS:	500	1000	1500	20	900	580

*** MARKET RESEARCH ***

BUSINESS INDEX THIS PERIOD: 100   FORECAST FOR NEXT PERIOD: 99
EST. OF AVERAGE SALES THIS PERIOD (IN UNITS): PANTS – 2700   TOPS – 900
ESTIMATE OF AVERAGE ADVERTISING LEVELS THIS QUARTER: $5000
PRICE & PRODUCT SURVEY (# FIRMS IN THIS LINE/AVG PRICE PANTS/AVG PRICE TOPS)
LINE 1: 1 /19.95/11.95 LINE 2: 0 / 0.00/0.00 LINE 3: 0 / 0.00/0.00
LINE 4: 0 / 0.00/0.00 LINE 5: 0 / 0.00/0.00

*** NEWS & MESSAGES ***

The National Retail Clothing Association survey indicated a very good holiday season. Sales were up an average of 14%. Due to the extremely good quarter, forecasts for the upcoming quarter indicate a slower period.

© 1987 Houghton Mifflin Company

interest based on 12% annual interest). The interest is calculated after your loan payment, if any, is applied to the outstanding balance.

Quarterly Profits. Your quarterly profits reflect all revenues and expenses for the quarter except your loan principal repayment. Principal repayments do not count as a valid expense for income tax purposes; therefore, your net receipts for the quarter are a more accurate reflection of all of your transactions for the quarter.

Loan Repayment. The bank will automatically issue loans to you to cover your immediate cash needs. These will be repaid automatically each quarter by a principal payment of $2,500. In addition, you will be charged 3% of the remaining balance as interest.

Balance Sheet

The balance sheet provided is very abbreviated. It shows the assets of the business and the claims on or ownership of those assets. Your balance sheet includes only current assets: cash, certificates of deposit, and inventory. Since all of your property and fixtures are leased, no fixed assets are shown. Your liabilities include all of your unpaid loans (liabilities), outstanding stock (equity) based on your original investment, and retained earnings from the income and expense statement. The equity and retained earnings are your total net worth (which is sometimes termed *owners' equity*).

Inventory Analysis

Production and Operations Management.   Retail stores have a "production" function similar to that of manufacturing companies. This function is called *operations management.* The raw materials or "inputs" are the store, the salespeople, and the merchandise. The outputs are the sales generated.

By keeping a close look at the inventory analysis on the quarterly report, you can monitor your inventory and develop more effective purchasing practices. Efficient inventory management will minimize your cost while providing an attractive array of goods to the consumer. The beginning inventory shown is the merchandise that was left from previous quarters. The products ordered reflect goods ordered for this quarter; the sum of these two represent merchandise available for sale. Shrinkage

© 1987 Houghton Mifflin Company

is the amount of goods that had to be disposed of because they were lost, were stolen, or became shopworn. The actual sales for the quarter are subtracted from merchandise available for sale less shrinkage; the ending inventory reflects the goods that are on the shelves at the end of each quarter.

The following is an example of the pants inventory information provided each quarter:

	Units
Beginning inventory (goods left over from previous period)	1,000
Merchandise purchased for this quarter	3,000
Total goods available for sale	4,000
Shrinkage (see explanation below)	− 50
Sales this quarter	−2,700
Ending inventory	1,250

Information on the inventory of tops is presented in the same way.

Carrying Costs.   One important aspect to be considered is the cost of carrying inventory from one quarter to another. In a business like yours, clothing can become soiled, go out of fashion, or go out of season. In any of these cases, the merchandise might be sold at greatly reduced prices or returned to the supplier for a substantial handling charge.

Due to the expenses associated with carrying merchandise from one quarter to another, you will want to determine the amount of inventory actually needed to make your establishment attractive without having too much inventory on hand. It may take several quarters for your team to develop a sense for the "right" level for your operation. The ending inventory will also affect the amount of cash in your checking account. Since the units remaining in inventory were paid for in the quarter in which they were ordered, a large inventory will strain the business's cash position while a small inventory will add to the cash available. Your cash balance can be verified on the Cash Account Verification Form found in Chapter 4.

Shrinkage.   Any time merchandise is displayed on open shelves and available for customer handling, there is the possibility that it will be soiled, stolen, lost (getting swept into the waste can, perhaps), or perhaps returned for credit after being worn. Sometimes goods are continually put back on shelves, into drawers, or into the stock room until they have gone out of season and it is even too late to have an end-of-season sale.

© 1987 Houghton Mifflin Company

In this case the merchandise will be given to a charitable institution. The total of such merchandise will be listed as shrinkage. It is assumed that no monies are received for these units. They are simply written off the inventory at their cost.

Your firm will need to track the shrinkage carefully to determine the possible cause(s). If there is not enough sales help on the floor, there is a greater chance of shoplifting. If inventory levels are kept too high, there is a greater chance of soiling or damage and of units being misplaced until they've gone out of season.

Market Research

The simulation will provide a Business Index for the current quarter and a forecast for the coming quarter. The Business Index is an indicator of consumer demand; one point reflects approximately 1% change in available demand. For example, a change in the index from 100 to 102 indicates that available demand has increased by about 2%. Of course, you must have the proper mix of price, advertising, and promotion to capture all of this available increase. In addition, this section of the quarterly report will provide an estimate of average sales, an estimate of average advertising levels, and the results of any surveys that you have purchased.

News & Messages

The News & Messages section of your quarterly report will provide messages from your instructor, describe the impact of your incident response, and offer other operational information—including warnings. Monitor this section of your report carefully so that you can make full use of the information contained in it.

Stock Price

In order to give participating teams some idea of how they are doing, the price of their common stock will be published each quarter. Although the company is actually "private" (that is, the stock does not sell actively on the open market), it will be assumed the stock sells on the over-the-counter market in order to assign a market value to the shares.

© 1987 Houghton Mifflin Company

The market value of your stock is not a *precise* indicator of the performance of your store, but it does give a rough estimate of the relative
standings of he competing firms. Since stock market investors apply
many nonquantifiable factors in valuing stock, you should not take the
stock price as an absolute indicator. It is, rather, an overall picture of the
relative simulation standings. After all, investor whims as a result of poor
performance in one quarter could make the stock price decline perhaps
more than it should. Investors may not know the firm's overall plans and
what it is trying to accomplish and thus may undervalue the stock. The
point is that you need to continue to operate your store as best you can
regardless of the stock price!

Some of the factors that affect stock price are:

1. Total sales
2. Return on sales (that is, profit divided by total sales)
3. Customer satisfaction (as reflected by the ability to maintain an
   optimum inventory and enough sales help on the floor)
4. Store image (as reflected by community social responsibility and
   advertising/promotion activities)

© 1987 Houghton Mifflin Company

3

DECISION INCIDENTS

This chapter contains twelve incidents, one for each decision period. A decision period equals one quarter (three months). The incidents are numbered to correspond with the same quarter. For example, Incident 1 is for the first quarter, Incident 2 is for the second quarter, and so on. The opportunity to purchase a piece of equipment or participate in a special event will be limited to the quarter in which it is offered.

© 1987 Houghton Mifflin Company

INCIDENT 1

The store you have purchased is located near a college campus. The location appeals to the student body and there is a fair amount of trade from surrounding neighborhoods. At $3,700 per quarter the rent is a bargain, and the previous owners have been moderately successful here. You have an option to lease space in a shopping center in a newly developed subdivision. The rent there is $6,000 per quarter, which includes a moderate amount of free advertising through flyers distributed by the shopping center Merchants Association. Both locations provide adequate parking, free exterior maintenance, and interior fixtures. Your lease expires at the end of this quarter. What should you do?

1. Stay in your present location.
2. Move to the shopping center.

Enter a 1 or 2 on line 11 of your decision form.

Note. It is not intended that either location will be a "bad" location. The location decision should be based on your motif, product line, and potential customers. This opportunity will not be available later in the simulation.

© 1987 Houghton Mifflin Company

INCIDENT 2

At the National Retailers Association annual convention, you saw a demonstration of a shoplifting prevention system. This system consists of removable tags to put on your more costly merchandise; if the tags pass a scanner installed at the entrance to the store, a warning alarm is sounded. The tags are easily attached and removed and leave no marks on the clothing. The manufacturer claims that the $5,000 cost of the system will be offset by the decrease in shoplifting (reported on the quarterly report as part of the shrinkage rate).

Other possibilities for increased security shown at the meeting include large mirrors mounted from the ceiling and closed circuit television cameras sweeping the sales floor. What action should you take? (Any costs will be automatically charged to Other Expenses.)

1. Buy the shoplifting prevention system. Cost $5,000.
2. Do not buy the system but put a warning sign in your front window stating that the premises are protected by a nonuniformed security guard. (Not true, but it may scare some would-be shoplifters.) Cost $50.
3. Do not buy the system but put a warning sign in your front window stating that the premises are protected by an "ultrasound laser security system." (Not true, but it may scare some would-be shoplifters; it does sound impressive doesn't it!) Cost $50.
4. Install large convex mirrors in the store. Cost $1,000.
5. Install two closed-circuit television cameras that continually sweep the area. Cost $2,000.
6. Do both 4 and 5 above. Total cost $3,000.
7. Do 1, 4, and 5 above. Total cost $8,000.
8. Do nothing. Your shrinkage is at the industry average. Also consider that such devices are insulting to the type of clientele that patronizes your store.

Enter a 1, 2, 3, 4, 5, 6, 7, or 8 on line 11 of the decision form.

Class Discussion Points. What level of expense should be devoted to "risk management"? Do warnings of protection trigger crimes? Should the business assume that consumers are honest or dishonest?

© 1987 Houghton Mifflin Company

INCIDENT 3

A local school official has just left your store. He has offered to name your store as the school system's official approved source for cheerleader, band, and pep club uniforms. He said the current supplier has not been doing a very good job of ordering and delivering clothing for these organizations. The usual procedure is for the individual student to come to the store, order the clothing, and place a small deposit to assure the clothing will be picked up. The store calls in the order to a specialty clothing manufacturer who ships the goods within two working days.

A call to the manufacturing firm confirms its ability to supply a high quality line at a reasonable price and guarantee two-day shipping "most of the time." Since the student makes a nonrefundable deposit when ordering, your shipping costs will be covered even if the clothing is not picked up. Although the supplier will not take back these custom-manufactured goods, you feel you can keep the merchandise in stock and sell it to another student within a short period of time. A quick mental calculation determines that you would increase profits by at least $3,000 for the coming year if you became the school's supplier; in fact, profits could be over $5,000 if a club or two changed uniform design and all new uniforms had to be ordered!

It seemed like a dream come true until the school official finished his explanation. "Of course, since I will be arranging all of this and encouraging clubs to buy from you... it's like I was working for YOU.... I would certainly hope you would buy me a nice birthday present. After all, I couldn't take money from you since I am working for the school system! But I don't want to give you the wrong idea—the birthday present would be only if you wanted to—there is no pressure involved. I guess other store owners would want to be friends with me if given the same opportunity!"

When asked what he would like for his birthday, he replied, "Well, I've always wanted to belong to the Windward Country Club." What should you do?

1. Give the official a membership to the country club. This would assure you of the school's endorsement. Cost $1,500.
2. Open an account at your store for the official with a credit of $1,000 in the hope that this will be a large enough "present" to win the system's endorsement. (You know it will only cost you half this amount, since your normal markup is 100%.)

© 1987 Houghton Mifflin Company

3. Open an account at your store for the official with a credit of $500 in the hope that this will be a large enough "present" to win the system's endorsement. (You know it will only cost you half this amount, since your normal markup is 100%.)
4. Turn down the offer and report the official to authorities.
5. Turn down the offer and take no other action.

Enter a 1, 2, 3, 4, or 5 on line 11 of the decision form.

Class Discussion Points. Is this a bribe? Should businesses engage in fee-splitting activities? If someone refers business to you, must you produce an in-kind payment? What is your social responsibility to the community that employs this person?

© 1987 Houghton Mifflin Company

INCIDENT 4

Recently, you noticed that one of your excellent employees was pushing a particular line of clothing exceptionally hard. Although you were suspicious, this person's sales record has been good and your customers seem pleased with him. Today you overheard a conversation between your employee and a sales representative and observed cash changing hands. This transaction indicated conclusively that your employee was being paid for promoting that particular line of clothing.

Your employee is an excellent salesperson whose volunteer activities in the local community have brought him a large following. For this reason, he has been offered a job by a nearby competitor. You feel certain that if you confront the situation, he will quit and go to work for your competitor. What action should you take?

1. Speak tactfully with the employee, explaining that you cannot allow this practice to continue. If the employee continues the practice, you are prepared to discharge him.
2. Speak tactfully with the employee, explaining that you cannot allow the practice to continue. You have already decided that he is too valuable to lose and will take no further action even if he continues to take the kickback.
3. Fire the employee explaining that kickbacks are illegal and unethical.
4. Do nothing.
5. Talk with the sales representative privately and tell him to stop this practice. It will be up to him to explain why he is ceasing this practice.
6. Post a notice on the employee bulletin board outlining the store's practice of prohibiting kickbacks; you hope this indirect approach will stop the practice without causing your salesperson to leave.
7. Choose option 1 above and give the employee in question a $1.00 per hour raise to help persuade him to remain with your store.

Enter a 1, 2, 3, 4, 5, 6, or 7 on line 11 of the decision form.

Class Discussion Points.   What are your responsibilities to your suppliers? To your other employees? To your customers? Can you control supplier behavior? How? Employee behavior? How?

© 1987 Houghton Mifflin Company

INCIDENT 5

One of your closest competitors has recently offered off-quality merchandise at extremely low prices. She has been advertising a large sale on "designer" or "brand-name" merchandise. The ads state that the price is "below normal cost" or "a buy-out price," and the price appears in the ads to be well below the usual cost of high-quality, brand-name goods.

However, when customers get to this competitor's store and compare the sale merchandise to the regular merchandise, they realize the quality is not the same and usually end up buying the regular line which has the normal markup. The competitor is smart enough to mix a few (very small size) designer-label goods in with the sale merchandise so she can claim that actual designer and brand-name merchandise is on sale. She knows that the general public expects some behavior of this type from retailers and feels the benefits are greater than the occasional backlash.

While this is sometimes referred to as bait-and-switch tactics, many retailers consider it to be an acceptable business practice and would respond "everyone does it." The pressure of the competitor's "special sales" are beginning to hurt your business somewhat. What should you do?

1. Try the same tactics for a short period to see if your customers object to the practice.
2. In order to keep up with the competition, you will conduct the same type of "sale" one or two times a month.
3. In order to keep ahead of the competition, you will conduct an ongoing "sale" of this type with a permanent table in a prominent place in the store.
4. Reject this practice and report your competitor (anonymously) to your local Bureau of Illegal Practices.
5. Reject this practice and attempt to get your competitor ejected from the retail clothing merchants association.
6. Reject this practice and advertise that you don't conduct such sales. State the reasons why your merchandise is worthy of consumer confidence.
7. Reject this practice and take no further action. You do not need to employ these practices; your advertising, the quality of your merchandise, and the expertise of your salespeople are all you need for success.

© 1987 Houghton Mifflin Company

Enter 1, 2, 3, 4, 5, 6, or 7 on line 11 of the decision form.

Class Discussion Points.   What responsibility does a merchant have to the consumer? Does the fact that something is a "common business practice" make that practice ethical? Acceptable? Is there a difference? Should there be?

© 1987 Houghton Mifflin Company

INCIDENT 6

Your regular suppliers are the vendors for a large garment manufacturer. Their product lines are well known, well advertised, and of moderate quality. Recently you were approached by a small garment cooperative located in a town about 100 miles from you. This co-op represents many small shops in homes and store fronts around the area. Called by the trade a "cottage industry," they produce a look-alike product of very high quality. You may choose to have their label placed in the clothing, or they will place your own label in the merchandise (private labeling). Moreover, the cost is 10% less than what you are currently paying.

Your current line from the large manufacturers provides name recognition and residual benefit from their brand advertising and offers the occasional opportunity to participate in cooperative ad campaigns (e.g., "Buy Goldensmith slacks at the following locations..."). The cottage operation provides a better product at a lower price and employs people who have been dislocated by manufacturing shutdowns. You have checked with other (out-of-town) stores that have been purchasing from this new source, and they report that they are very happy with the price, delivery, and especially the quality of the goods.

However, they also report that it takes a little longer to gain consumer acceptance with nonbranded goods. Some of the stores have ordered labels that look similar to those of the nonbranded goods and are having them placed in the clothing. Others seem to like the ego trip of having their store's own name placed in the garments.

You may contract to purchase a specific percentage of your goods from this new source. The simulation program will automatically include this source in your regular quarterly order. This proportion will be billed to you at 10% less than the cost of your regular line. Once the contract is signed, you may neither cancel the contract nor change the percentage of goods purchased for the balance of the simulation. (This "rule" is not derived from real life; it is intended to keep the simulation relatively uncluttered.) What action should you take?

1. Continue ordering through your regular suppliers. Place a 1 for the incident on the decision form.
2. Order _____ % of your total quarterly purchases from this source. The minimum amount you may order is 10% and the maximum is 90%.

© 1987 Houghton Mifflin Company

Enter a 1 or the percentage of goods ordered (as a whole number) from the new supplier on line 11 of the decision form. Be sure not to enter a decimal amount for the percentage (in other words, enter 20 for 20%).

Class Discussion Points. What should you consider when choosing a supplier? Are customers sensitive to minor differences in quality? How important is name recognition? Does the business have a social responsibility to support the development of "replacement" industries that employ dislocated workers?

© 1987 Houghton Mifflin Company

INCIDENT 7

The Committee to Reelect Senator Boasting has approached you to contribute toward the senator's reelection campaign. Boasting is the chairman of the Highway Committee and, if reelected, has promised (privately) to support a major new highway construction project in the vicinity of your store. If he is reelected and the highway project is approved, the increased traffic might raise your sales as much as 25%. The residents in the neighborhood are perturbed about the proposal because they feel that it would greatly change the residential environment and traffic patterns.

Knowledgeable sources have indicated that if the senator is reelected, the new project is almost a certainty. What action should you take?

1. Contribute $10,000. This would put the senator's campaign over the hump and his reelection would be almost assured.
2. Contribute $5,000. Probability is 60% that he would be reelected.
3. Contribute $1,000. Probability is 40% that he would be reelected.
4. Do not contribute to his campaign.

Enter a 1, 2, 3, or 4 on line 11 of the decision form.

Class Discussion Points. What are the issues to be considered in making political contributions? Is a political contribution a bribe? Are there ethical considerations that should be weighed before making a contribution that can lead to higher revenues?

© 1987 Houghton Mifflin Company

INCIDENT 8

In the past quarter you have noticed a slight decrease in sales during the hour in which you leave the store for lunch. One of your better part-time employees has been in charge during this period, and you had no reason until recently to suspect that the employee was dishonest. Then two incidents raised your suspicions.

While you were out for a movie one evening, you met one of the employee's teenagers and noticed the clothes she wore were from your store. Since employees receive a 20% discount on purchases, you are aware of all employee purchases and you know the clothes worn by the teenager had not been purchased by the employee. Yesterday when you returned from lunch you noticed about $40.00 lying on the shelf of the cash register. When you asked the employee why the money had not been rung up, the reply was "I got so busy I didn't have time." At this point you began to put together all the preceding single events and came to the conclusion that you could have a very dishonest employee working for you.

An article you just read stated that employee theft accounted for more retail store losses than shoplifting! Recalling the article, you telephoned a friend who is a police officer. Her advice was "Dishonest employees don't reform. You'd better take action now!" This is a very tough decision for you, however, because the employee is a single parent attempting to raise two children without the other parent contributing any support. The community welfare agency and the employee's religious organization are contributing toward the family's living expenses. You got the employee through the continuing education division of the school system, which has a retail clerk training program. The work record, attendance, attitude, and sales record of the employee have been superior. What should you do?

1. Call your friend at the Police Department and ask her to help you interrogate the employee. Employee theft is just as serious a crime as shoplifting, and prompt, decisive action is called for to prevent other employees from thinking they could get away with it too.
2. Interrogate the employee yourself to see if you can detect whether the employee is guilty or not.
3. The evidence is strong enough to take action. Tell the employee that business has been off and you will have to lay him/her off "for a while." However, you have no intention of calling him/her back.

© 1987 Houghton Mifflin Company

4. Number 1 above and lay the employee off if he/she admits the theft.
5. Number 1 above and press charges if the employee does not admit the guilt but the police officer believes there is enough evidence to warrant it.
6. Number 2 above and lay the employee off if he/she admits the theft.
7. Number 2 above and press charges if the employee does not admit the guilt but the police officer feels there is enough evidence to warrant it.
8. Number 2 above and offer to allow the employee to make full restitution for the thefts while continuing to work for you.
9. Number 2 above and offer to allow the employee to make full restitution if he/she goes to work elsewhere. You will help to find the employee a job where he/she would have no contact with money or goods.
10. Notify the police and let them investigate.

Enter a 1, 2, 3, 4, 5, 6, 7, 8, 9, or 10 on line 11 of the decision form.

Class Discussion Points.   Is this an issue of legal responsibility? Social responsibility? What are the issues that the management should consider in deciding what action to take?

© 1987 Houghton Mifflin Company

INCIDENT 9

One of the wholesalers that furnishes you with a very well made and popular line of jeans has offered you a tremendous co-op advertising package. They will pay 50% of all advertising that features their line of clothing during the next quarter. For the purposes of the simulation, that means that each dollar you spend will be matched by a dollar from them, doubling the effectiveness of your advertising. Ordinarily you would not pass this opportunity up, but the wholesaler's recent promotions have featured handsome young men and voluptuous women in very suggestive poses. The clothes are too tight and are very revealing.

Feminist groups in other cities have branded the ads sexist, and several religious councils have objected to the appearance of the ads in local media. Your queries to customers, families, and friends have brought mixed responses:

"Everyone carries ads like that."
- "Some people in the community will be offended, why take a chance?"
- "You can't afford to turn down this chance at substantially increasing the advertising budget at no additional cost."
- "With the young clientele served by this store, you have a social responsibility not to feature such ads."

What action should you take?

1. Run all the ads the wholesaler will sponsor. This will effectively double the impact of your current advertising budget.
2. Run half the ads available in media and at times of the day that will not reach a young audience. This will add 25% effectiveness to your advertising budget.
3. Run a fourth of the ads in media and at times of day that will not reach a young audience. This will add 10%–15% effectiveness to your current ad budget.
4. Turn the offer down.

Enter a 1, 2, 3, or 4 on line 11 of the decision form.

Class Discussion Points.   To whom is the business accountable? What are the consequences of being offensive to special interest groups? Does cost reduction offset the chance of offending the community?

© 1987 Houghton Mifflin Company

INCIDENT 10

You have recently been flooded with requests for donations to community causes. Since your store has been in operation for some time, most people assume that it is now profitable and feel that it is time for you to become a "good citizen" by supporting worthwhile community needs. You have noticed that some of your competitors are active in these causes. Which of the following should you support?

- Neighborhood arts council; supports art activities including classes for youth, summer art activities. Cost $200.
- Little League baseball team; shirts will have your name on the back. Cost $300.
- Scholarship for needy minority high school student to attend the retailing program at a local technical school. The school has an excellent reputation and the student might be a prospective employee some day. Cost $500.
- United Appeal campaign. Your "fair share" based on one month's business is $100.
- Summer youth employment program; needy college youth will work 15 hours per week in your store doing clerical work, sales, and light clean-up. Cost $600.
- Sheriff's clean-air camp for disadvantaged children; the camp provides two-week sessions at a well-run facility. Cost $400.

Place the *total* amount of funds you want to expend for these activities on line 11 of the decision form.

Class Discussion Points. Does the business have an obligation to support the community or does the community "support" the business? At what point of profitability should the business contribute? How much is enough? Not enough? Too much? Are there any benefits to the business?

© 1987 Houghton Mifflin Company

INCIDENT 11

The local college celebrates football homecoming each year with an elaborate parade and other festivities. Your store has been asked to participate by sponsoring a float for the Homecoming Queen's Court. The float will cost $2,000 to build. Moreover, you and your present staff are fully utilized; participation in the parade would require that you hire one part-time employee to provide additional sales support.

On the other hand, merchants report that the exposure results in favorable publicity in the community. A national retail merchants association newsletter published findings recently indicating that employees seem to have increased satisfaction in their jobs when they participate in community events. This satisfaction translates into greater enthusiasm with customers and improved sales. The cost of the float is, nevertheless, of major concern to one of your stockholders. All costs will be charged to Other Expenses. What should your team do?

1. Pass on the homecoming parade; the December holiday season will improve sales and you are concentrating your efforts on a successful fall quarter.
2. Place an ad in the football program. Cost $100.
3. Hire the local flying service to pull a banner over the parade route with your store's ad on it. Cost $300.
4. Make a donation of $500 to the Athletic Association. This will give you a sign on their official float.
5. Build the float. The $2,000 will be charged to Other Expenses.

Enter 1, 2, 3, 4, or 5 on line 11 of the decision form.

Class Discussion Points. Who benefits from publicity? Is a project that enhances employee satisfaction valuable if it is not a revenue-generating activity?

© 1987 Houghton Mifflin Company

INCIDENT 12

Business has been good during the last three years and a new opportunity has arisen. Your local township government is planning a restoration project in the downtown area. The project includes a theater, restaurants, professional offices, and a small shopping strip of specialty stores. Although there is no guarantee of success, similar projects in other areas have proved to be sound business investments after a slow start-up period.

In order to open a second store, you will need to use the profits from your existing operation to provide working capital to carry you through the slow start-up period. The rent for adequate space is $7,000 per quarter and the Economic Development Commission has offered very favorable loan packages of $35,000 at 10% interest to businesses that locate in the project. Your clientele will be residents from nearby areas and people who work in the downtown area. If you open a second store, you will carry the same merchandise in both locations. What action should you take?

1. Open the second store with product line 1. Continue with your existing product line.
2. Open the second store with product line 2. Continue with your existing product line.
3. Open the second store with product line 3. Continue with your existing product line.
4. Open the second store with product line 4. Continue with your existing product line.
5. Open the second store with product line 5. Continue with your existing product line.
6. Pass on this option and seek expansion in local neighborhoods.
7. Pass on a second store at this time.

Enter a 1, 2, 3, 4, 5, 6, or 7 on line 11 of your decision form.

Class Discussion Points.   How risk averse are you? How risk averse are others on your team? Can a small business stay small and succeed? How much truth is there in the statement "If you're not growing, you're stagnating"?

© 1987 Houghton Mifflin Company

4

THE MANAGEMENT FUNCTION: PLANNING, ORGANIZING AND CONTROLLING

Many management texts describe the functions of a manager as *planning* what tasks need to be accomplished, *organizing* resources to accomplish the tasks, *directing* the accomplishment of the tasks, and *controlling* the tasks from inception to completion. This chapter will provide information and decision aids to help in the planning, organizing, and controlling functions.

ESTABLISHING PURPOSES, PLANS, AND OBJECTIVES

The establishment of a purpose, or mission, for your store is the first step in the strategic planning process. This *short* statement explains exactly what the organization should be doing and why it exists. It specifies the nature of the business and the markets served. An example might be: "To provide moderately priced clothes and accessories to support the lifestyle of young working professionals." Such a statement is broad enough to permit diversification while it provides an image of the store's position in the marketplace.

Objectives

Objectives specify the action commitments that are being made to achieve the organization's purpose. They describe the long-range results that the organization wishes to achieve. Objectives provide management with the direction needed for effective coordination of human, financial, physical, and information resources. They can also serve to motivate those in the organization and provide a basis for control processes.

Objectives should be established in the following areas:[1]

1. Innovation
2. Market (or industry) standing
3. Financial resources
4. Physical resources
5. Profitability
6. Management development
7. Personnel relations
8. Productivity
9. Social responsibility

[1] Drucker, Peter, *Management: Tasks, Responsibilities, and Practices* (New York: Harper & Row, 1974).

© 1987 Houghton Mifflin Company

Plans

Merely establishing objectives falls far short of completing the planning tasks. The management team must have a plan of action to accomplish the desired objectives. These plans have different names in different organizations including "action plans," "strategies," "tactical plans," and so on. For the purpose of this simulation, the term *action plan* will be used.

Policies

After the team has established the general direction that the store should take, specific day-to-day guidelines must be prepared. These statements are called *policies.* They guide daily activities while providing some latitude to the manager in his or her decision making. Policies should be established in all areas for which there are objectives. An example of a marketing policy in this simulation is: "The advertising and promotion budget will be 5% of the previous quarter's gross revenues." A personnel policy might state: "All part-time employees will receive the equivalent of one work week of vacation after one year." Routine decisions and continuity of business practices are facilitated by these policy statements.

Form 4.1 on page 47 will assist your team to prepare its plans for the operation of your store.

Company Log

In order to provide continuity of decisions, each team may want to keep a log containing some or all of the following items:

1. Written notes explaining the rationale of each quarter's decisions—forms for this log are found in Chapter 6
2. Organization chart
3. Objectives and policies
4. Copy of each quarter's decision form
5. Table showing each quarter's decisions and results—the Record of Quarterly Decisions is found in Chapter 6
6. Comparative charts, graphs, or tables indicating the following quarterly information:
   a. Break-even analysis

© 1987 Houghton Mifflin Company

     b. Cash position
     c. Dividends paid
     d. Profits and return on investment
     e. Advertising/promotion expenditure
     f. Price
     g. Inventory position: beginning, purchases, ending
     h. Shrinkage
7. Copy of the quarterly report printout
8. Copy of the justification of the incident decision for each quarter
9. Any other information that would be of help in operating the firm

Many different types of forms and charts are included in this manual to help the management team maintain the records needed for good decision making.

© 1987 Houghton Mifflin Company

FORM 4.1 MISSION, OBJECTIVES, PLANS, AND POLICIES

COMPANY NO. _____   INDUSTRY _____

Corporate Mission: _____

_____

_____

Objective 1: _____

_____

_____

    Action Plan: _____

    _____

    _____

    Policies: _____

    _____

    _____

Objective 2: _____

_____

_____

    Action Plan: _____

    _____

    _____

    Policies: _____

    _____

    _____

Objective 3: _____

_____

_____

    Action Plan: _____

    _____

    _____

    Policies: _____

    _____

    _____

Objective 4: _____

_____

_____

© 1987 Houghton Mifflin Company

Action Plan: _____

_____

_____

Policies: _____

_____

_____

Objective 5: _____

_____

_____

Action Plan: _____

_____

_____

Policies: _____

_____

_____

Objective 6: _____

_____

_____

Action Plan: _____

_____

_____

Policies: _____

_____

_____

Objective 7: _____

_____

_____

Action Plan: _____

_____

_____

Policies: _____

_____

_____

Objective 8: _____

_____

_____

© 1987 Houghton Mifflin Company

Action Plan: _____
_____
_____

Policies: _____
_____
_____

Organizing

Each team should prepare an organization chart depicting the division
of tasks for the managers and employees. In a small business such as
yours, the owner(s) frequently act as managers, bookkeepers, buyers,
and salespeople. Your chart should reflect the roles that your staff
assumes at the store; each person may assume more than one role. The
following is an example of a two-person team of owners with two full-
time and two part-time salespersons:

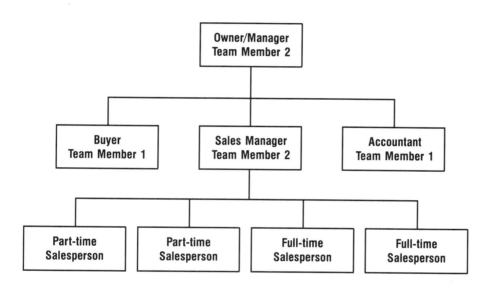

When teams are considering the best way to organize human and financial resources, they will need to consider where the personnel, marketing,
purchasing, and other departmental activities should be located.

Controlling

The management processes are not complete until there is some way to
analyze the outcomes of operations. This is the *control* function of
management. One method of accomplishing this is through an internal
management audit. This audit lets you review your store's results over
a certain period of time (generally four quarters, or one year), compare
them with your plans for the simulation when you started, and make

© 1987 Houghton Mifflin Company

any changes that you deem desirable in order to improve your performance and your own learning experience.

If this audit occurs at the midpoint of the simulation, you will have the opportunity to take corrective action. If it occurs at the end, your conclusions will be a "report card" of your success. This audit differs from an accounting audit in that you will be concerned with management issues as well as with variances from planned revenues and expenses.

The audit process begins by reviewing the stated missions, objectives, action plans, and policies for your store. Even if you did not write them down at the beginning of the simulation, you may ask yourself, "What was our original strategy? Are we still on course?" The next step is to measure your progress toward the achievement of this plan. Teams usually find it helpful to chart their revenues and expenses so they can monitor fluctuations more easily. Review the decision log. Do your decisions serve to implement your plans? How might you have done things differently? The Management Audit form on page 53 will provide a guide to conducting a management audit. As part of the audit procedure, you should also complete the Executive Bonus Recommendation form and the Business Simulation Peer Evaluation.

© 1987 Houghton Mifflin Company

FORM 4.2 MANAGEMENT AUDIT

Completed at the end of QUARTER NO. _____

COMPANY NO. _____   INDUSTRY _____

1. Does your store have an adequately stated mission, objectives, plans, and policies?

2. Did your team make decisions on a rational basis or did you take a "stab in the dark"?

3. How many times did your store have a low ending inventory that caused you to lose sales?

4. How many times did you overdraw your checking account at the bank and have to obtain a short-term loan?

5. Are you carrying excess inventory? Have you been able to attain an optimal ordering pattern for your level of sales?

6. Are you advertising and promoting enough? Too much? Can you determine a point of diminishing return?

7. Do you have sufficient sales staff to service your customers?

© 1987 Houghton Mifflin Company

8. Does your product line appeal to your market? Would another line of goods be more appropriate? Explain.

9. Do your business practices reflect your personal ethics and commitment to social responsibility? Has any incident created a "significant emotional event"? Did any of the incident responses cause you to rethink your attitudes and beliefs regarding social responsibility?

10. Should team members switch roles to enhance the learning experience? If so, what changes will you make?

11. (Final audit only) What advice would you give to a group of entrepreneurs who are opening a similar store in a nearby city?

© 1987 Houghton Mifflin Company

FORM 4.3 EXECUTIVE BONUS RECOMMENDATION

COMPANY No. _____

As a member of your company's Executive Compensation Committee, you have been assigned the task of allocating $50,000 among the managers.

Note. A fair, firm, and objective performance evaluation is a crucial managerial function. While peer evaluation is not easy, your instructor expects you to complete this task honestly.

Fill in names of the executives in your firm, including your own	*Fill in the amount of the executive bonus*
_____	$ _____
_____	$ _____
_____	$ _____
_____	$ _____
_____	$ _____
Total	$ 50,000

Your name _____

© 1987 Houghton Mifflin Company

FORM 4.4 BUSINESS SIMULATION PEER EVALUATION
COMPANY NO. _____

The purpose of this analysis is to give credit to those students who went the "extra mile" or who did their fair share in the simulation work. Conversely, if any team member did not do their fair share (for whatever reason) then that student should not get full credit for the simulation work. Be assured that all data on this form will be held in confidence.

Performance evaluation is an important part of every manager's job; your instructor expects you to make a fair and accurate evaluation.

NAMES (Your name on the first line)	ATTENDANCE & COOPERATION (5, 4, 3, 2, 1)	ACADEMIC CONTRIBUTION (5, 4, 3, 2, 1)	OVERALL COMPARATIVE RANKING (5, 4, 3, 2, 1)	TOTAL POINTS
_____	(Do not grade yourself but do rank yourself)		_____	
_____	_____	_____	_____	_____
_____	_____	_____	_____	_____
_____	_____	_____	_____	_____
_____	_____	_____	_____	_____

Add the points from the three columns and place in TOTAL POINTS column.

KEY TO NUMERICAL RANKING

ATTENDANCE & COOPERATION:
5 = Was a team leader both in and outside class; cooperation superior
4 = Attended meetings regularly; good cooperation; a team player
3 = Attended meetings fairly regularly; did what was asked but no more
2 = Missed some meetings and did the minimum amount of work
1 = Poor attendance at meetings and/or poor cooperation and work share

ACADEMIC CONTRIBUTION:
5 = A team leader in ideas; enthusiastic; a lot of good ideas
4 = Contributed greatly to the team; did more than his/her fair share
3 = Had good ideas from time to time; an average performance
2 = Probably was either too quiet or slightly disinterested to be an effective academic contributor to the team
1 = Contributed little to the team

OVERALL COMPARATIVE RANKING:
5 = THE TEAM LEADER (or A team leader, if more than one)
4 = A team player, second to the leader(s) only slightly; Excellent work
3 = An average member of the team
2 = Slightly below average member of the team
1 = Least contributor on the team

© 1987 Houghton Mifflin Company

FORM 4.5 QUARTERLY BUDGET VARIANCE

COMPANY NO. _____ QUARTER _____ INDUSTRY _____

SALES REVENUES   *Planned*   *Actual*

1. Units slacks sold _____ @ $ _____ = $ _____ $ _____
2. Units tops sold _____ @ $ _____ = $ _____ $ _____
3. Interest income $ _____ $ _____

Total revenues and interest (1, 2, & 3) $ _____ $ _____

EXPENSES

3. Total slacks ordered _____ @ $ _____ = $ _____ $ _____
4. Total tops ordered _____ @ $ _____ = $ _____ $ _____
5. Regular labor $ _____ $ _____
6. Part-time labor $ _____ $ _____
7. Advertising and promotion $ _____ $ _____
8. Rent and utilities $ _____ $ _____
9. Telephone and insurance $ _____ $ _____
10. Bank charges $ _____ $ _____
11. Market research $ _____ $ _____
12. Loan payments $ _____ $ _____
13. Interest payments $ _____ $ _____
14. Shrinkage $ _____ $ _____
15. Other expenses $ _____ $ _____

   Total expenses and loan payments
   (add 3–15) $ _____ $ _____

   Net Receipts $ _____ $ _____

© 1987 Houghton Mifflin Company

FORM 4.5 QUARTERLY BUDGET VARIANCE

COMPANY NO. _____ QUARTER _____ INDUSTRY _____

SALES REVENUES   *Planned*   *Actual*

1. Units slacks sold   _____ @ $ _____ = $ _____ $ _____
2. Units tops sold   _____ @ $ _____ = $ _____ $ _____
3. Interest income $ _____ $ _____

Total revenues and interest (1, 2, & 3) $ _____ $ _____

EXPENSES

  3. Total slacks ordered   _____ @ $ _____ = $ _____ $ _____
  4. Total tops ordered   _____ @ $ _____ = $ _____ $ _____
  5. Regular labor $ _____ $ _____
  6. Part-time labor $ _____ $ _____
  7. Advertising and promotion $ _____ $ _____
  8. Rent and utilities $ _____ $ _____
  9. Telephone and insurance $ _____ $ _____
10. Bank charges $ _____ $ _____
11. Market research $ _____ $ _____
12. Loan payments $ _____ $ _____
13. Interest payments $ _____ $ _____
14. Shrinkage $ _____ $ _____
15. Other expenses $ _____ $ _____

    Total expenses and loan payments
    (add 3–15) $ _____ $ _____

    Net Receipts $ _____ $ _____

© 1987 Houghton Mifflin Company

FORM 4.5   QUARTERLY BUDGET VARIANCE

COMPANY NO. _____   QUARTER _____   INDUSTRY _____

SALES REVENUES				*Planned*	*Actual*
1. Units slacks sold	_____ @ $ _____	= $ _____			$ _____
2. Units tops sold	_____ @ $ _____	= $ _____			$ _____
3. Interest income		$ _____			$ _____

Total revenues and interest (1, 2, & 3) $ _____ $ _____

EXPENSES

				Planned	*Actual*
3. Total slacks ordered	_____ @ $ _____	= $ _____			$ _____
4. Total tops ordered	_____ @ $ _____	= $ _____			$ _____
5. Regular labor		$ _____			$ _____
6. Part-time labor		$ _____			$ _____
7. Advertising and promotion		$ _____			$ _____
8. Rent and utilities		$ _____			$ _____
9. Telephone and insurance		$ _____			$ _____
10. Bank charges		$ _____			$ _____
11. Market research		$ _____			$ _____
12. Loan payments		$ _____			$ _____
13. Interest payments		$ _____			$ _____
14. Shrinkage		$ _____			$ _____
15. Other expenses		$ _____			$ _____

Total expenses and loan payments
(add 3–15) $ _____ $ _____

Net Receipts $ _____ $ _____

© 1987 Houghton Mifflin Company

FORM 4.5 QUARTERLY BUDGET VARIANCE

COMPANY NO. _____   QUARTER _____   INDUSTRY _____

SALES REVENUES			Planned	Actual
1. Units slacks sold	_____ @ $ _____	= $ _____	$ _____
2. Units tops sold	_____ @ $ _____	= $ _____	$ _____
3. Interest income		$ _____	$ _____

Total revenues and interest (1, 2, & 3) $ _____ $ _____

EXPENSES

			Planned	Actual
3. Total slacks ordered	_____ @ $ _____	= $ _____	$ _____
4. Total tops ordered	_____ @ $ _____	= $ _____	$ _____
5. Regular labor		$ _____	$ _____
6. Part-time labor		$ _____	$ _____
7. Advertising and promotion		$ _____	$ _____
8. Rent and utilities		$ _____	$ _____
9. Telephone and insurance		$ _____	$ _____
10. Bank charges		$ _____	$ _____
11. Market research		$ _____	$ _____
12. Loan payments		$ _____	$ _____
13. Interest payments		$ _____	$ _____
14. Shrinkage		$ _____	$ _____
15. Other expenses		$ _____	$ _____

Total expenses and loan payments
(add 3-15) $ _____ $ _____

Net Receipts $ _____ $ _____

© 1987 Houghton Mifflin Company

FIGURE 4.1   A SAMPLE CASH BUDGET ANALYSIS FOR QUARTER 1

QUARTER NO. _____   COMPANY NO. _____

INCOMING CASH

1. Revenues from sales for Quarter 1
   2700 jeans sold @ $19.95 $ 53,865
    900 tops sold @ $11.95 $ 10,755
2. Interest income $ 0

     3. Total Revenues (1 + 2) $ 64,620

4. Cash balance from previous quarter $ 0
5. Proceeds from stock sale &/or loan
   ($65,000 in qtr 1) $ 65,000

     Total available cash for expenses
     (3 + 4 + 5) $ 139,620

OUTGOING CASH FROM EXPENSES

Cost of inventory purchased
   3,000 jeans purchased @ $10.00 $ 30,000
   1,000 tops purchased @ $ 6.00 $ 6,000
Advertising & Promotion $ 5,000
Purchase price of business & rent deposit
   (Quarter 1 only – $65,000) $ 65,000
Salaries and wages
   Manager and 1 salesperson $ 15,000
   _____# add'l salespersons @ $900 each $ _____
Payroll taxes
   $15,000 total wages X 10% $ 1,500
Quarterly rent and utilities $ 3,700
Telephone & Insurance ($1,500 at start) $ 1,500
Interest on loans (3% of loan balance) $ 750
Bank charges $ _____
Other Expenses $ _____
Market Research $ 700
Shrinkage $ 1,000 (est.)
Estimated taxes (30% of profits) $ 2,000
Payment on loan principal $ 2,500
Dividend paid $ _____

     Total cash needed for expenses $ 129,620
     Net Cash This Quarter = Cash Available – Cash Needed = $ – 5,030

© 1987 Houghton Mifflin Company

FORM 4.6 CASH BUDGET ANALYSIS

QUARTER NO. _____   COMPANY NO. _____

INCOMING CASH

1. Revenues from sales for Quarter _____
   _____ jeans sold @ $ _____._____ $ _____
   _____ tops sold @ $ _____._____ $ _____
2. Interest income $ _____

    3. Total Revenues (1 + 2) $ _____

4. Cash balance from previous quarter $ _____
5. Proceeds from stock sale &/or loan
   ($75,000 in qtr 1) $ _____

    Total available cash for expenses
    (3 + 4 + 5) $ _____

OUTGOING CASH FROM EXPENSES

Cost of inventory purchased
    _____ jeans purchased @ $ _____._____ $ _____
    _____ tops purchased @ $ _____._____ $ _____
Advertising & Promotion $ _____
Purchase price of business & rent deposit
    (Quarter 1 only – $65,000) $ _____
Salaries and wages
    Manager and 1 salesperson $ _____
    _____ # add'l salespersons @ $900 each $ _____
Payroll taxes
    $ _____ total wages × 10% $ _____
Quarterly rent and utilities $ _____
Telephone & Insurance ($1,500 at start) $ _____
Interest on loans (3% of loan balance) $ _____
Bank charges $ _____
Other Expenses $ _____
Market Research $ _____
Shrinkage $ _____
Estimated taxes (30% of profits) $ _____
Payment on loan principal $ _____
Dividend paid $ _____

    Total cash needed for expenses $ _____
    Net Cash This Quarter = Cash Available – Cash Needed = $ _____

© 1987 Houghton Mifflin Company

FORM 4.6 CASH BUDGET ANALYSIS

QUARTER NO. _____   COMPANY NO. _____

INCOMING CASH

1. Revenues from sales for Quarter _____
   _____jeans sold @ $ _____._____ $ _____
   _____tops sold @ $ _____._____ $ _____
2. Interest income $ _____

    3. Total Revenues (1 + 2) $ _____

4. Cash balance from previous quarter $ _____
5. Proceeds from stock sale &/or loan
   ($75,000 in qtr 1) $ _____

    Total available cash for expenses
    (3 + 4 + 5) $ _____

OUTGOING CASH FROM EXPENSES

Cost of inventory purchased
        _____jeans purchased @ $ _____._____ $ _____
        _____tops purchased @ $ _____._____ $ _____
Advertising & Promotion $ _____
Purchase price of business & rent deposit
    (Quarter 1 only – $65,000) $ _____
Salaries and wages
    Manager and 1 salesperson $ _____
    _____# add'l salespersons @ $900 each $ _____
Payroll taxes
    $ _____total wages × 10% $ _____
Quarterly rent and utilities $ _____
Telephone & Insurance ($1,500 at start) $ _____
Interest on loans (3% of loan balance) $ _____
Bank charges $ _____
Other Expenses $ _____
Market Research $ _____
Shrinkage $ _____
Estimated taxes (30% of profits) $ _____
Payment on loan principal $ _____
Dividend paid $ _____

    Total cash needed for expenses $ _____
    Net Cash This Quarter = Cash Available – Cash Needed = $ _____

© 1987 Houghton Mifflin Company

FORM 4.6 CASH BUDGET ANALYSIS

QUARTER NO. _____   COMPANY NO. _____

INCOMING CASH

1. Revenues from sales for Quarter _____
   _____ jeans sold @ $ _____ . _____ $ _____
   _____ tops sold @ $ _____ . _____ $ _____
2. Interest income $ _____

   3. Total Revenues (1 + 2) $ _____

4. Cash balance from previous quarter $ _____
5. Proceeds from stock sale &/or loan
   ($75,000 in qtr 1) $ _____

   Total available cash for expenses
   (3 + 4 + 5) $ _____

OUTGOING CASH FROM EXPENSES

Cost of inventory purchased
   _____ jeans purchased @ $ _____ . _____ $ _____
   _____ tops purchased @ $ _____ . _____ $ _____
Advertising & Promotion $ _____
Purchase price of business & rent deposit
   (Quarter 1 only – $65,000) $ _____
Salaries and wages
   Manager and 1 salesperson $ _____
   _____ # add'l salespersons @ $900 each $ _____
Payroll taxes
   $ _____ total wages × 10% $ _____
Quarterly rent and utilities $ _____
Telephone & Insurance ($1,500 at start) $ _____
Interest on loans (3% of loan balance) $ _____
Bank charges $ _____
Other Expenses $ _____
Market Research $ _____
Shrinkage $ _____
Estimated taxes (30% of profits) $ _____
Payment on loan principal $ _____
Dividend paid $ _____

   Total cash needed for expenses $ _____
   Net Cash This Quarter = Cash Available – Cash Needed = $ _____

© 1987 Houghton Mifflin Company

FORM 4.6 CASH BUDGET ANALYSIS

QUARTER NO. _____   COMPANY NO. _____

INCOMING CASH

1. Revenues from sales for Quarter _____
   _____ jeans sold @ $ _____ . _____ $ _____
   _____ tops sold @ $ _____ . _____ $ _____
2. Interest income $ _____

   3. Total Revenues (1 + 2) $ _____

4. Cash balance from previous quarter $ _____
5. Proceeds from stock sale &/or loan
   ($75,000 in qtr 1) $ _____

   Total available cash for expenses
   (3 + 4 + 5) $ _____

OUTGOING CASH FROM EXPENSES

Cost of inventory purchased
   _____ jeans purchased @ $ _____ . _____ $ _____
   _____ tops purchased @ $ _____ . _____ $ _____
Advertising & Promotion $ _____
Purchase price of business & rent deposit
   (Quarter 1 only – $65,000) $ _____
Salaries and wages
   Manager and 1 salesperson $ _____
   _____ # add'l salespersons @ $900 each $ _____
Payroll taxes
   $ _____ total wages × 10% $ _____
Quarterly rent and utilities $ _____
Telephone & Insurance ($1,500 at start) $ _____
Interest on loans (3% of loan balance) $ _____
Bank charges $ _____
Other Expenses $ _____
Market Research $ _____
Shrinkage $ _____
Estimated taxes (30% of profits) $ _____
Payment on loan principal $ _____
Dividend paid $ _____

   Total cash needed for expenses $ _____
   Net Cash This Quarter = Cash Available – Cash Needed = $ _____

© 1987 Houghton Mifflin Company

FIGURE 4.2 A SAMPLE CASH ACCOUNT VERIFICATION FORM FOR QUARTER 0

The main purpose of this form is to demonstrate the impact of net changes in inventory on the cash position. If purchases are greater than sales, then cash will be depleted by the amount of the difference. On the other hand, if sales are greater than purchases, then cash will be increased by the amount of the difference.

QUARTER NO. _*0*_   COMPANY NO. _*X*_

This form shows the effect of inventory levels on the cash position.

1. Last quarter cash		$ 1,650
2. Net revenues this quarter		$ 32,220
Changes in Inventory:		
Beginning slacks inventory this qtr (in units)	1,000	
Less ending slacks inventory this qtr (in units)	1,250	
Net inventory change (in units)**	−250	
times unit COST each	X 10.00	
3. *Net inventory change in slacks ($)***		$ −2,500
Beginning tops inventory this qtr (in units)	500	
Less ending tops inventory this qtr (in units)	580	
Net inventory change (in units)**	−80	
times unit COST each	X 6.00	
4. *Net inventory change in tops ($)***		$ −480
5. Sum 1, 2, 3, 4 (subtract any negative numbers)		$ 30,890
6. Total expenses for the quarter	−	$ 29,350
7. Dividends paid	−	$ 500
8. Loan payment	−	$ 0
Subtract 6, 7, 8 from 5 = Checking Acct. Balance		$ 1,040

**These may be negative numbers; if so, subtract these numbers from the sum.

© 1987 Houghton Mifflin Company

FORM 4.7 CASH ACCOUNT VERIFICATION FORM

QUARTER NO. _____   COMPANY NO. _____

This form shows the effect of inventory levels on the cash position.

1. Last quarter cash $ _____
2. Net revenues this quarter $ _____

    Changes in Inventory:
    Beginning slacks inventory this qtr (in units)   _____
    Ending slacks inventory this qtr (in units)   _____
        Net inventory change (in units)**   _____
            times unit COST each   ✗ _____.____

3. *Net inventory change in slacks ($)*** $ _____

    Beginning tops inventory this qtr (in units)   _____
    Ending tops inventory this qtr (in units)   _____
        Net inventory change (in units)**   _____
            times unit COST each   ✗ _____.____

4. *Net inventory change in tops ($)*** $ _____
5. Sum 1, 2, 3, 4 (subtract any negative numbers) $ _____
6. Total expenses for the quarter   − $ _____
7. Dividends paid   − $ _____
8. Loan payment   − $ _____

    Subtract 6, 7, 8 from 5 = Checking Acct. Balance $ _____

© 1987 Houghton Mifflin Company

**These may be negative numbers; if so, subtract these numbers from the sum.

FORM 4.7 CASH ACCOUNT VERIFICATION FORM

QUARTER NO. _____   COMPANY NO. _____

This form shows the effect of inventory levels on the cash position.

1. Last quarter cash $ _____
2. Net revenues this quarter $ _____

    Changes in Inventory:
    Beginning slacks inventory this qtr (in units)   _____
    Ending slacks inventory this qtr (in units)   _____
       Net inventory change (in units)**   _____
          times unit COST each   X _____.___

3. *Net inventory change in slacks* ($)** $ _____

    Beginning tops inventory this qtr (in units)   _____
    Ending tops inventory this qtr (in units)   _____
       Net inventory change (in units)**   _____
          times unit COST each   X _____.___

4. *Net inventory change in tops* ($)** $ _____
5. Sum 1, 2, 3, 4 (subtract any negative numbers) $ _____
6. Total expenses for the quarter   – $ _____
7. Dividends paid   – $ _____
8. Loan payment   – $ _____

    Subtract 6, 7, 8 from 5 = Checking Acct. Balance $ _____

© 1987 Houghton Mifflin Company

**These may be negative numbers; if so, subtract these numbers from the sum.

FORM 4.7 CASH ACCOUNT VERIFICATION FORM

QUARTER NO. _____   COMPANY NO. _____

This form shows the effect of inventory levels on the cash position.

1. Last quarter cash $ _____
2. Net revenues this quarter $ _____

    Changes in Inventory:
    Beginning slacks inventory this qtr (in units)   _____
    Ending slacks inventory this qtr (in units)   _____
       Net inventory change (in units)**   _____
          times unit COST each   × _____.___

3. *Net inventory change in slacks ($)*** $ _____

    Beginning tops inventory this qtr (in units)   _____
    Ending tops inventory this qtr (in units)   _____
       Net inventory change (in units)**   _____
          times unit COST each   × _____.___

4. *Net inventory change in tops ($)*** $ _____
5. Sum 1, 2, 3, 4 (subtract any negative numbers) $ _____
6. Total expenses for the quarter   − $ _____
7. Dividends paid   − $ _____
8. Loan payment   − $ _____

    Subtract 6, 7, 8 from 5 = Checking Acct. Balance $ _____

© 1987 Houghton Mifflin Company

**These may be negative numbers; if so, subtract these numbers from the sum.

FORM 4.7 CASH ACCOUNT VERIFICATION FORM

QUARTER NO. _____   COMPANY NO. _____

This form shows the effect of inventory levels on the cash position.

1. Last quarter cash $ _____
2. Net revenues this quarter $ _____

   Changes in Inventory:
   Beginning slacks inventory this qtr (in units)   _____
   Ending slacks inventory this qtr (in units)   _____
     Net inventory change (in units)**   _____
       times unit COST each   X _____.____

3. *Net inventory change in slacks ($)*** $ _____

   Beginning tops inventory this qtr (in units)   _____
   Ending tops inventory this qtr (in units)   _____
     Net inventory change (in units)**   _____
       times unit COST each   X _____.____

4. *Net inventory change in tops ($)*** $ _____
5. Sum 1, 2, 3, 4 (subtract any negative numbers) $ _____
6. Total expenses for the quarter   – $ _____
7. Dividends paid   – $ _____
8. Loan payment   – $ _____

    Subtract 6, 7, 8 from 5 = Checking Acct. Balance $ _____

© 1987 Houghton Mifflin Company

**These may be negative numbers; if so, subtract these numbers from the sum.

5

INVENTORY, RATIOS, AND BREAK-EVEN ANALYSIS

INVENTORY MANAGEMENT WORKSHEET

The Inventory Management and Break-even Worksheet will assist you in projecting a cost-effective amount of inventory. It will not assure you of sufficient stock, nor will it prevent occasional excesses. In general, a higher number reflects better inventory management as long as the merchandise on hand is sufficient to entice customers. Sparse stock can be unattractive. See the example below.

1. Forecasted sales this quarter   4000 units
2. Ending inventory last quarter   500 units
3. Targeted ending inventory this quarter   1200 units

$$\text{Inventory turnover} = \frac{\text{Sales}}{\text{Avg. Inv.}}$$

$$\frac{\text{Item 1}}{(\text{Item 2} + \text{Item 3})/2} = \text{Inventory Turnover}$$

$$\frac{4000}{(500 + 1200)/2} = 4.7 \text{ times}$$

BREAK-EVEN ANALYSIS

In order to help establish prices and determine how much inventory to purchase, a business must analyze the relationship between costs, profit, and sales. The point at which the cost of operations equals the revenues from sales is called the break-even point. Owners of retail businesses are concerned with the volume of product sold (i.e., the number of units) that produces break-even as well as the dollar amount of sales necessary to break even. In order to make this determination, it is necessary to separate the fixed (ongoing) costs from the variable costs associated with each unit of product. The variable costs in this case are the cost to purchase the product.

In this simulation, the fixed costs of $28,120 apply to both products. However, the slacks sell for approximately twice the price of the tops and a greater number are sold. Therefore, in this example, 87.5% of the fixed costs will be allocated to slacks and 12.5% will be allocated to tops. The prices are assumed to be $20 for the slacks and $12 for the tops. Break-even volume can now be calculated for each product:

© 1987 Houghton Mifflin Company

Slacks

$$\text{Break-even volume} = \frac{.875 \times \text{(fixed costs)}}{\text{unit price} - \text{unit cost}} = \frac{.875 \times 28,120}{20 - 10} = 2,461 \text{ pairs}$$

Tops

$$\text{Break-even volume} = \frac{.125 \times \text{(fixed costs)}}{\text{unit price} - \text{unit cost}} = \frac{.125 \times 28,120}{12 - 6} = 586 \text{ tops}$$

Note.   Fixed costs include salaries and wages, payroll taxes, rent and utilities, telephone and insurance, advertising and promotion, interest expense, market research, and other expenses. (Loan payments and taxes are not considered to be fixed costs.)

© 1987 Houghton Mifflin Company

FORM 5.1 INVENTORY MANAGEMENT AND BREAK-EVEN ANALYSIS

COMPANY NO. _____   QUARTER NO. _____

INVENTORY MANAGEMENT

1. Forecasted sales this quarter   _____

2. Ending inventory last quarter   _____

3. Targeted ending inventory this quarter   _____

Inventory turnover:

$$\frac{\text{Item 1}}{(\text{Item 2} + \text{Item 3})/2} = \text{Inventory Turnover}$$

$$\underline{\hspace{4cm}} = \underline{\hspace{2cm}} \text{ times}$$

BREAK-EVEN ANALYSIS

Slacks

$$\text{Break-even volume} = \frac{.875 \times \text{fixed costs}}{\text{unit price} - \text{unit cost}} = \underline{\hspace{2cm}} = \underline{\hspace{1.5cm}} \text{ pairs}$$

Tops

$$\text{Break-even volume} = \frac{.125 \times \text{fixed costs}}{\text{unit price} - \text{unit cost}} = \underline{\hspace{2cm}} = \underline{\hspace{1.5cm}} \text{ tops}$$

© 1987 Houghton Mifflin Company

FORM 5.1 INVENTORY MANAGEMENT AND BREAK-EVEN ANALYSIS

COMPANY NO. _____   QUARTER NO. _____

INVENTORY MANAGEMENT

1. Forecasted sales this quarter   _____

2. Ending inventory last quarter   _____

3. Targeted ending inventory this quarter   _____

Inventory turnover:

$$\frac{\text{Item 1}}{(\text{Item 2} + \text{Item 3})/2} = \text{Inventory Turnover}$$

$$\text{_____} = \text{_____ times}$$

BREAK-EVEN ANALYSIS

Slacks

$$\text{Break-even volume} = \frac{.875 \times \text{fixed costs}}{\text{unit price} - \text{unit cost}} = \text{_____} = \text{_____ pairs}$$

Tops

$$\text{Break-even volume} = \frac{.125 \times \text{fixed costs}}{\text{unit price} - \text{unit cost}} = \text{_____} = \text{_____ tops}$$

© 1987 Houghton Mifflin Company

FORM 5.1 INVENTORY MANAGEMENT AND BREAK-EVEN ANALYSIS

COMPANY NO. _____   QUARTER NO. _____

INVENTORY MANAGEMENT

1. Forecasted sales this quarter   _____

2. Ending inventory last quarter   _____

3. Targeted ending inventory this quarter   _____

Inventory turnover:

$$\frac{\text{Item 1}}{(\text{Item 2} + \text{Item 3})/2} = \text{Inventory Turnover}$$

$$\underline{\hspace{3cm}} = \underline{\hspace{2cm}} \text{ times}$$

BREAK-EVEN ANALYSIS

Slacks

$$\text{Break-even volume} = \frac{.875 \times \text{fixed costs}}{\text{unit price} - \text{unit cost}} = \underline{\hspace{1.5cm}} = \underline{\hspace{1.5cm}} \text{ pairs}$$

Tops

$$\text{Break-even volume} = \frac{.125 \times \text{fixed costs}}{\text{unit price} - \text{unit cost}} = \underline{\hspace{1.5cm}} = \underline{\hspace{1.5cm}} \text{ tops}$$

© 1987 Houghton Mifflin Company

FORM 5.1   INVENTORY MANAGEMENT AND BREAK-EVEN ANALYSIS

COMPANY NO. _____   QUARTER NO. _____

INVENTORY MANAGEMENT

1. Forecasted sales this quarter   _____

2. Ending inventory last quarter   _____

3. Targeted ending inventory this quarter   _____

Inventory turnover:

$$\frac{\text{Item 1}}{(\text{Item 2} + \text{Item 3})/2} = \text{Inventory Turnover}$$

$$\underline{\hspace{4cm}} = \underline{\hspace{3cm}} \text{ times}$$

BREAK-EVEN ANALYSIS

Slacks

$$\text{Break-even volume} = \frac{.875 \times \text{fixed costs}}{\text{unit price} - \text{unit cost}} = \underline{\hspace{2cm}} = \underline{\hspace{2cm}} \text{pairs}$$

Tops

$$\text{Break-even volume} = \frac{.125 \times \text{fixed costs}}{\text{unit price} - \text{unit cost}} = \underline{\hspace{2cm}} = \underline{\hspace{2cm}} \text{tops}$$

© 1987 Houghton Mifflin Company

FIGURE 5.1   EXAMPLE OF COMPLETED SELECTED RATIOS FORM

COMPANY NO. _____   INDUSTRY _____

SELECTED RATIOS
for Quarter No. 0

PREPARED BY _____

1. INVENTORY TURNOVER (Indicates efficient inventory management)

$$\frac{\text{Units Sold (Tops)}}{\text{* (Beg. inv. + End. inv.)}/2} = \frac{900}{(500 + 580)/2} = 1.67$$

2. GROSS PROFIT MARGIN (Describes the relationship between the cost of buying goods and the amount of sales generated. It is an indication of how your price is affecting profitability.)

$$\frac{\text{Sales \$ - Cost of Goods Sold}}{\text{Sales \$}} = \frac{64,620 - 32,400}{64,620} = .499$$

3. RETURN ON SALES (Describes the relationship between all expenses of operations and sales revenues generated. It is an indication of how costs are affecting profitability.)

$$\frac{\text{Quarterly Profits}}{\text{Total Sales \$}} = \frac{2,870}{64,620} = .04$$

4. ADVERTISING AS A % OF SALES (Provides a benchmark for understanding the relationship between advertising and sales. Generally should be compared to an industry average.)

$$\frac{\text{Total Adv. \& Promo. \$}}{\text{Total Sales \$}} = \frac{5,000}{64,620} = .077$$

5. SALES REVENUE PER DOLLAR OF EMPLOYEE TIME (Provides a benchmark for understanding the relationship between employee efficiency and sales.)

$$\frac{\text{Total Quarterly Sales \$}}{\text{Total Wages \& Salaries}} = \frac{64,620}{15,000} = 4.31$$

6. OVERHEAD AS A % OF SALES (Provides a benchmark for understanding the costs involved in generating a given level of sales.)

$$\frac{\text{Total Overhead}}{\text{Total Quarterly Sales \$}} = \frac{28,120}{64,620} = .435$$

© 1987 Houghton Mifflin Company

*Average Inventory

FORM 5.2 SELECTED RATIOS

COMPANY NO. _____   INDUSTRY _____

SELECTED RATIOS

Quarter No. _____

PREPARED BY _____

1. INVENTORY TURNOVER

$$\frac{\text{Units Sold}}{\text{* (Beg. inv. + End. inv.)}/2} = \underline{\hspace{3cm}} =$$

2. GROSS PROFIT MARGIN

$$\frac{\text{Sales \$ - Cost of Goods Sold}}{\text{Sales \$}} = \underline{\hspace{3cm}} =$$

3. RETURN ON SALES

$$\frac{\text{Quarterly Profits}}{\text{Total Sales \$}} = \underline{\hspace{3cm}} =$$

4. ADVERTISING AS A % OF SALES

$$\frac{\text{Total Adv. \& Promo. \$}}{\text{Total Sales \$}} = \underline{\hspace{3cm}} =$$

5. SALES REVENUE PER DOLLAR OF EMPLOYEE TIME

$$\frac{\text{Total Quarterly Sales \$}}{\text{Total Wages \& Salaries}} = \underline{\hspace{3cm}} =$$

6. OVERHEAD AS A % OF SALES

$$\frac{\text{Total Overhead}}{\text{Total Quarterly Sales \$}} = \underline{\hspace{3cm}} =$$

* Average Inventory

© 1987 Houghton Mifflin Company

FORM 5.2 SELECTED RATIOS

COMPANY NO. _____   INDUSTRY _____

SELECTED RATIOS
Quarter No. _____

PREPARED BY _____

1. INVENTORY TURNOVER

$$\frac{\text{Units Sold}}{\text{* (Beg. inv. + End. inv.)/2}} = \underline{\hspace{5cm}} =$$

2. GROSS PROFIT MARGIN

$$\frac{\text{Sales \$ - Cost of Goods Sold}}{\text{Sales \$}} = \underline{\hspace{5cm}} =$$

3. RETURN ON SALES

$$\frac{\text{Quarterly Profits}}{\text{Total Sales \$}} = \underline{\hspace{5cm}} =$$

4 ADVERTISING AS A % OF SALES

$$\frac{\text{Total Adv. \& Promo. \$}}{\text{Total Sales \$}} = \underline{\hspace{5cm}} =$$

5. SALES REVENUE PER DOLLAR OF EMPLOYEE TIME

$$\frac{\text{Total Quarterly Sales \$}}{\text{Total Wages \& Salaries}} = \underline{\hspace{5cm}} =$$

6. OVERHEAD AS A % OF SALES

$$\frac{\text{Total Overhead}}{\text{Total Quarterly Sales \$}} = \underline{\hspace{5cm}} =$$

© 1987 Houghton Mifflin Company

* Average Inventory

FORM 5.2 SELECTED RATIOS

COMPANY NO. _____   INDUSTRY _____

SELECTED RATIOS

Quarter No. _____

PREPARED BY _____

1. INVENTORY TURNOVER

$$\frac{\text{Units Sold}}{\text{* (Beg. inv. + End. inv.)/2}} = \underline{\hspace{4cm}} =$$

2. GROSS PROFIT MARGIN

$$\frac{\text{Sales \$ − Cost of Goods Sold}}{\text{Sales \$}} = \underline{\hspace{4cm}} =$$

3. RETURN ON SALES

$$\frac{\text{Quarterly Profits}}{\text{Total Sales \$}} = \underline{\hspace{4cm}} =$$

4. ADVERTISING AS A % OF SALES

$$\frac{\text{Total Adv. \& Promo. \$}}{\text{Total Sales \$}} = \underline{\hspace{4cm}} =$$

5. SALES REVENUE PER DOLLAR OF EMPLOYEE TIME

$$\frac{\text{Total Quarterly Sales \$}}{\text{Total Wages \& Salaries}} = \underline{\hspace{4cm}} =$$

6. OVERHEAD AS A % OF SALES

$$\frac{\text{Total Overhead}}{\text{Total Quarterly Sales \$}} = \underline{\hspace{4cm}} =$$

© 1987 Houghton Mifflin Company

* Average Inventory

FORM 5.2 SELECTED RATIOS

COMPANY NO. _____   INDUSTRY _____

SELECTED RATIOS

Quarter No. _____

PREPARED BY _____

1. INVENTORY TURNOVER

$$\frac{\text{Units Sold}}{\text{* (Beg. inv. + End. inv.)/2}} = \text{_____} =$$

2. GROSS PROFIT MARGIN

$$\frac{\text{Sales \$ - Cost of Goods Sold}}{\text{Sales \$}} = \text{_____} =$$

3. RETURN ON SALES

$$\frac{\text{Quarterly Profits}}{\text{Total Sales \$}} = \text{_____} =$$

4. ADVERTISING AS A % OF SALES

$$\frac{\text{Total Adv. \& Promo. \$}}{\text{Total Sales \$}} = \text{_____} =$$

5. SALES REVENUE PER DOLLAR OF EMPLOYEE TIME

$$\frac{\text{Total Quarterly Sales \$}}{\text{Total Wages \& Salaries}} = \text{_____} =$$

6. OVERHEAD AS A % OF SALES

$$\frac{\text{Total Overhead}}{\text{Total Quarterly Sales \$}} = \text{_____} =$$

© 1987 Houghton Mifflin Company

* Average Inventory

6

WORKSHEETS AND
DECISION FORMS

This chapter contains forms and worksheets to summarize your quarterly decisions and the decision form that will be used to enter the simulation decision.

© 1987 Houghton Mifflin Company

© 1987 Houghton Mifflin Company

FORM 6.1 RECORD OF QUARTERLY DECISIONS

Period No.	No. of Slacks Ordered	No. of Tops Ordered	Product Line	Price Slacks	Price Tops	Ad. & Promo. Expense	Part-time Staff	Payment Type	Mark. Res. $	Dividends	Inci-dent
0											
1											
2											
3											
4											
5											
6											
7											
8											
9											
10											
11											
12											

FORM 6.2 MARKETING DATA ANALYSIS

Period No.	Ad. & Promo. Budget	Price Tops	Price Slacks	Sales— Tops	Sales— Slacks	% Inc. (Dec.)	Ad/Sales Ratio
0							
1							
2							
3							
4							
5							
6							
7							
8							
9							
10							
11							
12							

© 1987 Houghton Mifflin Company

FORM 6.3 LOG OF QUARTERLY DECISIONS

COMPANY NO. _____   QUARTER NO. _____

Decision: _____
_____
_____

Rationale: _____
_____
_____
_____

Decision: _____
_____
_____

Rationale: _____
_____
_____
_____

Decision: _____
_____
_____

Rationale: _____
_____
_____
_____

Decision: _____
_____
_____

Rationale: _____
_____
_____
_____

© 1987 Houghton Mifflin Company

Decision: _____
_____
_____

Rationale: _____
_____
_____
_____

© 1987 Houghton Mifflin Company

FORM 6.4 DECISION FORM

INDUSTRY _____   QUARTER NO. _____   COMPANY NO. _____

    1. Purchase # slacks (no commas)   _____

    2. Purchase # tops (no commas)   _____

    3. Line of clothing (1-5)   _____

    4. Price: slacks   _____ . _____

    5. Price: tops   _____ . _____

    6. Advertising & promotion (no commas)   _____

    7. Part-time sales staff (0-10)   _____

    8. Cash only (0); Cash & credit cards (1) _____

    9. Market research (0-$700)   _____

10. Dividends   _____

11. Incident   _____

    VERIFICATION TOTAL

****

Note. Add all the numbers you have inserted on lines 1 to 11. Place the total (including cents) in the verification box. This is used to verify correctness of the numbers as they are typed into the computer. The total MUST be correct or your instructor may fine you.

Members of the team present:

_____   _____

_____   _____

© 1987 Houghton Mifflin Company

FORM 6.4 DECISION FORM

INDUSTRY _____   QUARTER NO. _____   COMPANY NO. _____

    1. Purchase # slacks (no commas)   _____

    2. Purchase # tops (no commas)   _____

    3. Line of clothing (1-5)   _____

    4. Price: slacks   _____ . _____

    5. Price: tops   _____ . _____

    6. Advertising & promotion (no commas)   _____

    7. Part-time sales staff (0-10)   _____

    8. Cash only (0); Cash & credit cards (1)   _____

    9. Market research (0-$700)   _____

10. Dividends   _____

11. Incident   _____

        VERIFICATION TOTAL   [_____ . _____]

****

Note. Add all the numbers you have inserted on lines 1 to 11. Place the total (including cents) in the verification box. This is used to verify correctness of the numbers as they are typed into the computer. The total MUST be correct or your instructor may fine you.

Members of the team present:

_____   _____

_____   _____

© 1987 Houghton Mifflin Company

FORM 6.4 DECISION FORM

INDUSTRY _____   QUARTER NO. _____   COMPANY NO. _____

   1. Purchase # slacks (no commas)   _____

   2. Purchase # tops (no commas)   _____

   3. Line of clothing (1-5)   _____

   4. Price: slacks   _____ . _____

   5. Price: tops   _____ . _____

   6. Advertising & promotion (no commas) _____

   7. Part-time sales staff (0-10)   _____

   8. Cash only (0); Cash & credit cards (1) _____

   9. Market research (0-$700)   _____

10. Dividends   _____

11. Incident   _____

    VERIFICATION TOTAL | _____ . |

****

Note. Add all the numbers you have inserted on lines 1 to 11. Place the total (including cents) in the verification box. This is used to verify correctness of the numbers as they are typed into the computer. The total **MUST** be correct or your instructor may fine you.

Members of the team present:

_____   _____

_____   _____

© 1987 Houghton Mifflin Company

FORM 6.4 DECISION FORM

INDUSTRY _____   QUARTER NO. _____   COMPANY NO. _____

   1. Purchase # slacks (no commas)   _____

   2. Purchase # tops (no commas)   _____

   3. Line of clothing (1-5)   _____

   4. Price: slacks   _____ . _____

   5. Price: tops   _____ . _____

   6. Advertising & promotion (no commas)   _____

   7. Part-time sales staff (0-10)   _____

   8. Cash only (0); Cash & credit cards (1)   _____

   9. Market research (0-$700)   _____

10. Dividends   _____

11. Incident   _____

    VERIFICATION TOTAL   [_____ . ____]

****

Note. Add all the numbers you have inserted on lines 1 to 11. Place the total (including cents) in the verification box. This is used to verify correctness of the numbers as they are typed into the computer. The total MUST be correct or your instructor may fine you.

Members of the team present:

_____   _____

_____   _____

© 1987 Houghton Mifflin Company

FORM 6.4 DECISION FORM

INDUSTRY _____   QUARTER NO. _____   COMPANY NO. _____

   1. Purchase # slacks (no commas)   _____

   2. Purchase # tops (no commas)   _____

   3. Line of clothing (1-5)   _____

   4. Price: slacks   _____ . _____

   5. Price: tops   _____ . _____

   6. Advertising & promotion (no commas)   _____

   7. Part-time sales staff (0-10)   _____

   8. Cash only (0); Cash & credit cards (1)   _____

   9. Market research (0-$700)   _____

10. Dividends   _____

11. Incident   _____

     VERIFICATION TOTAL   [_____ . _____]

****

Note.   Add all the numbers you have inserted on lines 1 to 11. Place the total (including cents) in the verification box. This is used to verify correctness of the numbers as they are typed into the computer. The total MUST be correct or your instructor may fine you.

Members of the team present:

_____   _____

_____   _____

© 1987 Houghton Mifflin Company

FORM 6.4 DECISION FORM

INDUSTRY _____   QUARTER NO. _____   COMPANY NO. _____

    1. Purchase # slacks (no commas)   _____

    2. Purchase # tops (no commas)   _____

    3. Line of clothing (1–5)   _____

    4. Price: slacks   _____._____

    5. Price: tops   _____._____

    6. Advertising & promotion (no commas)   _____

    7. Part-time sales staff (0–10)   _____

    8. Cash only (0); Cash & credit cards (1)   _____

    9. Market research (0–$700)   _____

10. Dividends   _____

11. Incident   _____

    VERIFICATION TOTAL   [_____ . ____]

****

Note. Add all the numbers you have inserted on lines 1 to 11. Place the total (including cents) in the verification box. This is used to verify correctness of the numbers as they are typed into the computer. The total MUST be correct or your instructor may fine you.

Members of the team present:

_____   _____

_____   _____

© 1987 Houghton Mifflin Company